MW01102007

TIMBER
FRAME MASTERY

*A ROADMAP TO CREATE LASTING BEAUTY
HANDCRAFTED CONSTRUCTIONS*

JOSEPH BENTON

TABLE OF CONTENTS

INTRODUCTION

Making use of timber frame construction methods to build your own house used to be a niche in the self-construction market. Nonetheless, according to a 2017 report, the number of self-constructed timber frames (or SIPs) is now almost equal to the number of self-constructed buildings.

This is attributed, at least in part, to the factory quality and quick production time going in handy with the development of a timber frame house.

This beginner's timber frame construction guide discusses what it's like, how to choose the right system or manufacturer, what the rate includes, and how those costs stack up to maçonnery.

Timber frame construction of some sort is a technique that has been around for millennia. Nonetheless, over time, it has become a remarkably sophisticated process. Today's timber frame construction is unrecognizable when next to its predecessors.

While it's not ideal for every building scenario, due to the ability to prefabricate elements, timber frame construction has its own set of advantages in relation to alternative materials.

This guide will provide readers with a solid understanding of timber frame construction, and it also includes information on the benefits of its use, as well as how it can work with other building materials such as external cladding on brick walls.

Timber frame buildings are built to last, ensuring that there are still many historic timber-framed structures that are in use today.

1

HISTORY OF TIMBER FRAMING

Timber is such an excellent building material that its use is predated to be history, no wonder. A lot of cultures around the world capitalized on this building method. Here's the back story behind the timber framing development.

Creating a foundation of a timber frame requires engaging in a long tradition of architecture. Located in Europe, Middle East, Africa, and Asia archeological sites, timber framing has a global history.

Because of the robust, durable quality of the wood and the pure simplicity of the building, timber framing has been prevalent in construction works for thousands of years. It was used to build homes and construct other buildings all over the world, where trees are plentiful. Nevertheless, timber framing evolved differently in each area, due to differences in the services available in different regions, and it was even absent from some others. Deserts, Tundra, or the high Arctic are places where forests were scarce, so it was simply not possible to build timber frames or logs. Only certain parts of the world could have maintained a well-developed timber frame culture of vast and readily available woods. But there were many parts of the world where vast areas of forest-covered land provided excellent quality building timber.

For example, in India, as early as 200 BC, the joints used to create timber frame structures already existed: teak timbers molded and connected to basic joinery and bamboo pegs. Moreover, it is believed that the Jokhang Monastery in Lhasa, Tibet, is the world's oldest timber frame construction, dating back to the 7th century. Japanese builders also discovered the strength and durability of dealing with wooden joints and fibrous timbers. Stone buildings would crumble under pressure in an environment vulnerable to typhoons and earthquakes, while the woods shrugged and bore the weight. Not to mention the iconic Japanese timber framing marvel, the pagoda roof.

In Europe, since the Neolithic period, Timber has been used as a building material in UK buildings. Archeologists in England have found evidence of timber-framed dwellings dating over 10,000 years ago. Ancient stone monuments such as Stonehenge, made use of joinery features identical to the timber framing systems of today. Recently, timber framing experienced an increase in prominence during the Roman and Georgian eras. Timber framing has gained widespread popularity in the UK throughout history, as it was in high demand for shipbuilding until the

Victorian era. The timber was prevalent as a building material until the 16th century, thanks to Britain's wood supply of oak. The testament to its durability is that so many homes made with it still stand today.

Timber framing is the basis of English half-timbered houses (where the architectural timbers sit on the filled and stuccoes outside). Some of Europe's oldest wooden houses are located in England and Scotland, and today's earliest wood-framed structures in the UK date back to the 13th century.

Massive beams and posts bear the whole weight in a timber-frame building; wall sheathing is just a barrier used to hold in the water. In the 1960s, new timber frame building techniques were developed in the UK, and they are an entirely accepted construction technique.

In the United States, timber framing was the primary method from the 17th century to the mid-19th century for the design of wooden houses.

The frame of the wood was hewn by hand. All the frame timbers have been felled and squared by hand in the early days. Despite the fact that the advent sawmills power made it possible to make square timbers by machine, all the notching was still done by hand for the rather sophisticated joinery. House wrights should build their unique cuts to make joints and also attach timbers; the old houses have innovative variations of mortises and tenons, dovetails and other joints.

New timber framing has capitalized on innovation, leveraging manufacturing by automated mills in order to increase production and also reduce costs. Nevertheless, timber framing was a purely handcrafted operation from the ground up before the invention of the modern mill. Early American Diaries in New England describe the timber framing environment as one of community-driven work. Farmers in need of a new barn will spend the winter harvesting timber, they'll also spend the spring preparing the wood for a master wood frame. The farmer and his neighbors would construct the building together, under the direction of the timber framer. With the aid of fellow citizens, barns and town halls were designed quickly.

Timber framing was typical in the United States until the late 1800s. Nevertheless, technological inventions and the need to accommodate an increasing population helped in pushing aside this form of constructing. Sawmills started to manufacture rectangular timber, which was much more straightforward than large posts and beams to ship, cut, and build. Carpenters discovered that they could use inexpensive, factory-made nails to mount such "pins" into frameworks, where the building's weight was borne by the walls rather than a massive frame. The method, known as balloon framing, took far less expertise and time than using massive timbers. Timber framing was one of America's major building styles until the early 1900s, when the industrial revolution met housing demand by manufacturing lighter, rectangular timber from its new factories. Instead of timber frame construction, this style of lumber contributed to the development of "light frame" or "stick building," where the concrete structure is often made up of a series of small pieces of wood.

The timber frame made a house that was strong and durable. The invention of cheaper balloon construction (using machine-sawn lumber and iron nails), however, made the old custom look costly, and with builders, it soon fell out of favor. Until the 1970s, timber framing has been a common subset of custom new buildings.

Although stick framing remains the dominant home building firm in the U.S., timber framing began to revive in the 1970s, when a group of dedicated developers resurrected the style of the timber frame, and they began building classic design structures. Then, people have been fascinated by the artisan value of timber framing. Today, timber frame architecture provides the strength and elegance of the conventional timber frame, alongside separation, functionality, and several other changes. The disparity between the timber framing of today and 30 years ago can be attributed to the manufacture of computer-aided design (CAD) and computer numerical control (CNC). Such tools allow constructors to create designs and also proceed to production quickly.

Despite being out of favor in recent centuries, despite the advancements in other building techniques, timber has seen a resurgence in modern times, demonstrating the enduring popularity of timber frame houses.

Timber framers now combine modern construction technologies and engineering, so as to improve traditional methods.

If a house is an early timber frame is really impossible to tell from the outside. But inside, there are telling signs. The posts and beams of summer (i.e., tall, central) are so large that they often protrude from walls and ceilings. Such large timbers were often covered with beaded edges in flat planed panels. The casing was typically removed by later generations of "restorers," in order to expose the rough framing timbers, a practice that might have horrified some fastidious early occupants.

Before we go into the historic buildings created by Asian and American timber framing, let's take a closer look at different styles that remain in Europe.

Germany Tradition

Where else can you go on a holiday, based on houses with a timber frame, except Germany? The three thousand kilometers long timber frame path crossing the center of Germany connects the picturesque historic timber frame towns of Bavaria and Baden-Württemberg, with the diverse coastal regions along the shore of the North Sea. On your trip spanning hundreds of years from the early 1300s to the late 19th century, you will come across seven different types of timber frame, corresponding to the seven segments of the route. When you start your journey to the south of the country, you will find buildings in the Lower German timber frame, with large spaces on the ground floors which are separated into three sections of accommodation, a large hall, and bedrooms. For the mainly agricultural communities which are expanding through the fertile lands of lower Germany and as far south as Switzerland, this style worked well.

Farther north, you will see the shift in architectural style to well-preserved timber frames and half-timbered houses, reflecting the Central German tradition. A smaller footprint accommodates a balanced frame with a street-facing front room, backward kitchen, and bedrooms. Such multileveled structures suit the mountainous terrain well, and over the years, they have established a distinct high gabled look that features prominently in Germany's romantic fantasies of several visitors. Finally, as you get closer to the north of the country, you enter a region traditionally dominated by the proximity of the sea and the wealth of maritime trading, which has taken place over the centuries. The Upper German timber frame style presents the most diverse buildings that often vary from city to city. This diversity was primarily due to the material quality, as well as the distinctive construction technique introduced by craftsmen in the early Middle Ages, involving double framed beams and widely separated posts.

British Isles

England and Scotland have a long tradition of using wood as one of the most relevant construction materials. The classic shopping street of York, The Shambles, conjures up early medieval pictures, with its jetted upper levels protruding from the main buildings and partly covering the walkways below. Due to the modernization efforts of the 18th and 19th centuries, many timber frames and half-timbered structures were able to acquire a new façade. Nonetheless, the primary material that fills in the gaps between the wooden frame often remains the same: wattle and daub. For earlier timber frame construction, as well as a more economical option to bricks, daub filling consisted of a lattice of tiny wooden strips or sticks filled with a crumbly mixture of clay, dirt, and sand, which became a permanent filling process. A more prominent example of Tudor's half-timbered style would be hard to find other than Cheshire's Little Moreton Hall.

This enchanting manor house at the end of the 16th

century features traditional medieval design elements, such as herringbone patterning, oak beams, Elizabethan fireplaces, galleries with wood panels, as well as chevron and lozenge designs, covering the outer walls. By comparison, Wealden hall-type houses, prominent in the southeast of England, are designed by merchants and wealthy commoners with more utility in mind. A thatched roof and two central halls on either side of the fireplace, these multilevel structures often included jettied upper levels, which are there to support extended family life. A typical example of a dramatic past is the Old Punch Bowl in West Sussex, from the early 1400s.

Francophone Regions

In most parts of France and the surrounding regions, timber framing and half-timbered buildings are common. Timber framing in Normandy has a long history. The region's capital city, Rouen, has a variety of styles ranging over seven hundred years from different historical eras. The town provides a look back to the Middle Ages, from plain frames to intricate woodworking decorations. Over the years, artisans often use two main techniques: they dug the posts directly into the earth with the post-in-ground method, while they placed the posts on a beam laid on the place with the post-on-sill technique. Total timber constructions indicated also increased fire risk for most medieval towns, as well as the common practice of combining timber framing with stones and structural wall fillers. Half-timbered houses became a hallmark of Basque architecture in the 15th century, in the southern parts of France. While most architects tend to choose stone and brick to build the first floors, capital always fell along the way, and timber was an appropriate option to add a second level.

Jetted overhangs and extensions of the second story are commonplace in this region, as they have dark red and colorful blue paints. Barrie is the traditional half-timbered Basque building style that can be recognized by its moderately pitched roofs and its generous sizes designed to accommodate extended families. However, the Baserri was a central part of Basque culture, which symbolized communities in both northern Spain and southern France within the settlements.

Asia

Post and lintel building was one of the earliest ways used for constructing a framed opening, using various materials which include timber. Many of these constructions in different parts of Asia have been exceptionally well preserved, giving an insight to the ingenuity of timber framing. Also, today, the traditional Chinese gates that we have come to equate with Chinatowns in the major western cities are impressively essential ways of post and beam engineering: two beams planted in the ground,

client, but also for creating a new atmosphere, becoming the Biel city symbol."

Different Styles of Timber Framing

Italian, French, Basque, and English are just a few of the timber-framed house styles. During the 13th to 18th centuries, a proliferation of techniques came into play throughout Europe, with several regionally distinct styles developing.

Wernigerode Timber-framed town hall in Germany

Houses in Braubach in the 16th century

Homes in Rennes, Brittany, France

Notable Features of Timber Framing

Hardwood timbers are exceptionally durable material, and they can last for decades. As a result, there are still several outstanding medieval wooden doors.

Perhaps, one of the reasons that timber has been so prevalent throughout the centuries is that it is easy to work with, and it comes in a variety of shades to suit a vast array of styles, as shown by the various patterns that have arisen between different cultures and periods.

Recently, planners, developers, and Eco experts praised its green credentials as one of the only sustainable building materials.

The Modern Timber Revival

In the 1970s in the UK, as well as in the USA and Canada, where more inexpensive mass-produced technologies were widespread, timber-framed houses saw something of a resurgence. The methods were initially mediocre in performance, though, at least in the UK.

The timber was usually a poor quality softwood with little structural integrity. The structure was easily built with internal brick skin, and the final product was inferior overall, and it had a low-quality smell. That differed from some other countries where timber-framed buildings, one of which was Sweden, were still popular.

Swedish Superiority

Over the centuries, timber-framed buildings have remained popular in Sweden, and the Swedish artisans have improved their skills in building timber houses over the past 50 years. One of the reasons for the higher quality was the significant differences between the production of timber buildings by the Swedes and Scandinavians, compared to the British system.

They used a high-quality wood first and foremost. The timber used in Sweden has been growing slowly for over 50 years, compared to the UK, where forestry has been growing fast for over 25 years. That had a significant impact on the main product's structural integrity.

Throughout Sweden, as opposed to walls with door openings, artisans often preferred creating wall panels, beginning with the window and constructing a frame around it. It meant that with a factory finish, each panel had total thermal integrity.

In contrast, it was more common in the United Kingdom to find lightweight frames with window openings, which were then erected on-site and retrospectively fitted the windows. That made a weak part of the overall building of the junction between the windows and the frame.

Improvements in UK Timber Buildings

While the movement towards timber-framed buildings in the United Kingdom in the 1970s has done considerable damage to its image, we are now seeing a revival of the industry. For the construction of care homes, hospitals, and other houses, timber framing is now widely used. It generally provides a higher level of environmental quality, as it is an environmentally friendly method that is known for its energy efficiency.

Many UK companies have now opted to adopt many of the Scandinavians' talents, and they are building timber houses with excellent ecological quality and sustainability. Such structures can last for over 50 years, as long as they are well managed throughout their lives. Timber is likely to remain a popular and highly successful building material in the UK for several years to come, as long as the right methods are used.

2

AN OVERVIEW OF TIMBER STRUCTURES

WHAT IS TIMBER FRAME?

Timber is a variety of wood that has been converted into beams and boards. It is also known in the United States and Canada as "lumber." Timber or Lumber is simply a woodland or firewood with growing trees. Every wood that can yield a minimum size can also be considered as timber or lumber. It's a step in the wood production process. Timbers are the forests raised for architectural purposes. Finished wood is supplied to the market in standard sizes. Timber is commonly used for the construction of houses and furniture.

The modern timber framing is a method in house-building framed wood structures. The void between the 'skeleton' of the wood is filled with cement, rock, and filler, ensuring that the construction is extremely durable and also provides use for centuries.

Often, flexible energy-efficient and durable are beautifully built and elegant timber frame houses. Nonetheless, what makes the construction of timber so unique? In today's timber frame homes, we cover all you need to know about how modern design meets traditional craftsmanship.

Timber framing has been done for decades, and most of our homes and many of our smaller wooden buildings are still being constructed in North America. But, there are different ways that can be used to create the structure's frame or skeleton. Although light frame architecture involves some thin wooden sticks that are cut to length and also nailed together, a timber frame structure uses smaller, much larger pieces that are designed to lock together at their links.

Even when carefully constructed, light frame building is known to be rough carpentry, thereby causing finished walls and ceilings to hide it in dwellings. New timber frame construction, on the other hand, is usually exposed, and timbers can be prepared, as well as the craftsman's talent and care required. The timber-framed house of today combines the best of the old techniques with the benefits of the new structural integrity and energy efficiency.

It is also possible to integrate timber frame components into a log and stick frame designs, generating impressive visual appeal.

It is the manner of construction that separates this home-style from another. It has been around for decades, to begin with–a testament to their strength and durability. Inside, most look like more traditional buildings, or if you add more mountain architecture, you'll undoubtedly notice a difference in the light-exposed timber trusses on the outside. Within, however, a spectacular interior space is created by the artfully crafted timbers, trusses, and decorative timber accents, which are supported by wooden pegs. Timber has a unique style, extraordinary endurance, green nature, energy efficiency, and compelling personality. Custom timber frame homes provide fantastic design options and a close-to-nature feeling, which permeates these beautifully crafted homes, making a real connection from the outside in.

Timber Framing Defined

A timber frame is a wooden structure that is load-bearing, fixed together with mortise or tenon joinery. The post and beam construction is also similar to timber framing, but along with bolts and other steel connections, post and beam buildings are held, instead of wooden joints. Timber frames are cut in such a way that their ends fit like a puzzle, and wooden pegs hold the joinery faster. These pegs are made by hand, with draw knives, and they're torn from straight-grained hardwood stock.

Builders are no longer restricted from the use of hand tools. Nevertheless, there is a lot of variation in the layout and cutting of timber frames. Timber Homes strives to use both power and hand tools to work effectively. This is possible by using chain mortisers, plate saws, and chain saws to rough out our joinery. We aspire to have a manufacturing-oriented shop, as well as exclusive and cool pieces.

What's a Timber Home?

A timber home is a kind of house that uses a frame construction with substantial posts and beams, which are connected to pegs or other decorative joinery forms. The structure's walls are almost always mounted on the outside of the timber frame, leaving the timbers vulnerable to the visual effect. Timber framing is stiff, old, and so well-established that the building used to get the name of it. It forms the basis of a hundred-year-long building.

One of the significant advantages of timber frame construction is that it's so solid that it doesn't have to break load-bearing walls through the middle of the house. That means you can build the layout in any arrangement you like, including an open wide room/dining/kitchen/entry. On the other side, thanks to the heat of the wood and the joinery, the frame binds the volumes of transparent designs and brings them down to a more humane scale. The timber skeleton can also be painted in any way you want, in order for your timber house to look like any other house style and match anywhere.

The timber industry uses environmentally friendly and renewable raw materials, which provide an excellent environmental balance. Natural wood has many unique properties, and it is increasingly popular with commercial, public and private building owners.

The house uses various timber structures.

Wooden skeleton structures

Vertical braces or vertical cross-bars and pillars also form the supporting structure of a wooden frame. Reinforcing requires planks and other reinforcing components. Using grids and deploying solid structural timber, the wooden skeleton structure represents a wooden economic structure with large support clearances. Beam-laminated timber or board-laminated timber is as well used for extensive permissions.

We need to distinguish between primary and secondary supporting skeleton structures. As secondary supporting structures, the walls pass the vertical loads as the main supporting structures. These can be executed as single or multi-component structures. The walls themselves have no fixed purpose, and they can be organized and built at will. This construction method's advantage is: Large window areas and variable floor layouts can be easily realized. The skeleton structure is also reinforced by using wood-based materials in a vertical direction, and by the ceiling panels of the second supporting structure or a solid core.

Some examples are staircases or elevator shafts. Clearances of 1250x 1250 mm (49x49 inches) are preferred grid dimensions in wooden skeleton structures; a grid of 60 cm (Euro module) (23 inches) is also fitting and common.

The wooden skeleton frame is often used to construct building supporting warehouses, sporting halls, and swimming pools. In residential buildings, in a post and beam or wooden frame houses, we find skeleton structures. Here as well, the dynamic floor plan layout provides excellent benefits. Gypsum frame is plasterboard; however, wooden-based materials such as boards, are often used to support framework planking.

Wood frame construction

A prefabricated wooden frame composed of braces, levels, and top plates forms the basis of wooden frame construction. High-quality solid-built timber (KVH) is also used as a construction material. The frame is lined with plastic material at the factory or on the construction site. The wood frame construction is commonly used in prefabricated housing with high quantities of ready-made materials.

The load is moved by plate, and the engineered grid-shaped supports reinforce walls against buckling and bulging. A force-fit attachment of floor, ceiling, and roof structure panels guarantees the entire building's stability. Planking strengthens walls, and it undertakes essential construction-physics activities. Wall thermal insulation provides heat, vibration, and thermal protection.

62.5 cm (246 inches)multiples reflect an economic axis clearance as this length is consistent with most panel building materials. Wooden frame constructions have numerous benefits that make this form, especially attractive for housing construction. These include the good thermal insulation values, the weather-independent planning, and prefabrication possibilities, and the resulting short construction times. Lean wall superstructures also allow more living space in relation to solid houses, and the building owner can do a lot of the work themselves, thereby increasing construction costs.

Wooden frame construction varies with prefabrication quantity. Based on the maker, we can differentiate between three degrees:

Parts are transported to the construction site for full assembly, but the assembling is carried out solely on the construction site (wooden frame construction).

Semi-finished pieces were supplied as single sets. The force-fit link strengthens the frame during transportation.

Completely prefabricated sections are walls with planking on both ends, plus insulation. Partly, window components and building service equipment, or even the outside façade, may as well be included.

Together with wooden frame construction, they also speak of post and beam construction. The underlying design and building standards are mostly the same, but the post and beam structure varies primarily in the degree of prefabrication.

Log constructions

Initially, log walls made of tree trunks spread over each other. A construction method has emerged from these beginnings recently, which is high-quality and economical through a high degree of prefabrication. Prefabricated round logs are used to build solid log walls. In addition to traditional single-skinned wall construction, multi-layered constructions are also feasible.

The log house construction has several characteristics to be checked in order to prevent faulty installations. The specialized components, such as T-rails or slide fittings, consider the different settling properties of the components used. The settling must also be considered in multilayered wall buildings.

Double log walls, consisting of two log walls with an insulation layer between them, are popular. A two-framed log house walls consist of a log wall, namely (inside or outside) an insulation sheet and inside planking, or an outside curtain wall façade. Most times, the interior walls in a log house can be understood as log walls or drywall constructions. Also essential is a careful and professional joint execution. A log house has several joints. Leakages cause heat loss and should be stopped. Once a log house is built, improvements can only be enforced to a minimal extent. Changes should never be made without contacting the site planner or structural engineer.

Choose between various assembly combinations of log house construction. Main assemblies like foundations, multiple forms of design assembly, and self-assembly are possible. We give building owners their log house assembly, but it will be supervised by an accomplished master craftsman.

Nail Laminated Timber Construction

For nail-laminated timber constructions, two-dimensional structures made from softwood are used. Slats placed side-by-side, which can consist of boards, planks, and squared timber, are attached laterally for force-fit. Possible ways of attachment are doweling, nailing, and gluing. It produces solid wooden cross-sections, especially fire-resistant. Based on the component thickness, F30 to F90 fire resistance levels can also be obtained.

The static supporting structure consists of the wall elements, which, besides their weight, adsorb, and also pass vertical and horizontal loads. Based on the maker, the slats are between 24 to 60 mm (0,9 to 2,3 inches) thick. The walls and ceilings are framed with wooden-based materials for structural purposes, typically OSB panels that allow wall superstructure diffusion. To avoid contact with metal contacts or lack of dimensional integrity, the nail-lined timber walls are attached to wooden dowels and glued:

Glued nail-laminated wood can be sliced to any length. Even during variations in moisture content, the component size remains consistent, as deformations by swelling and shrinking are accounted for by slat joints.

Doweled wooden components are incredibly durable, as they are attached to Beechwood dowels. The dowels, mounted with 6%, swell in the softwood with lower wood humidity, and they lock the individual slats together irreversibly.

One benefit of building nail-laminated timber is that no grids are needed. Here, floor plans can be constructed quickly, and openings can also be incorporated at will. Generally, the wood deficit is tiny, as cut-outs can already be reused during processing. Nail-laminated wooden roofs work in combination with in-situ concrete; bird's heads, knacks, perforated plates, and screw ties operate as shear connectors. Once the structural component is mounted, it adsorbs the tensile forces and acts as the missing formwork. Concrete absorbs compressive pressures, and it provides sound insulation through its high weight. Such wooden-concrete components are often employed for wide-span structural ceilings; the ceiling elements are gradually prefabricated to avoid the intrusion of moisture on-site.

3

BENEFITS OF USING TIMBER FRAMES

Timber frame buildings have been around since ancient times. It's one of the oldest construction methods. If you want a house with plenty of open space and proper ventilation, you should go with timber frame homes. In today's world, there is a modern touch to it, and these people want to live in wholly modernized homes. Builders use timber frames to make the houses look elegant and trendy, along with some conventional touches. With the aid of these, you can model your homes to make them contemporary and traditional.

If you're looking for a cost-effective and environmentally friendly way of living, living in these houses is the best option. You can live comfortably without having further money. Such homes are relatively cheap, and if you want to build a timber frame house on your property, you can visit one of the firms ready to take up your plan in your town. Users can also get advice on how to build the right timber frame homes. With the correct internet search engine, you can get all the details you want and launch your project once you've done your research.

If you approach the right construction companies, you'll get all the help you need, and you'll end up more than satisfied with the results. Building your house will be finished within the given timeframe, and you can be confident that your desires and wishes will do the work. When making or buying these houses, you should take suitable safety measures as well.

The right thing for you is to retire and live in a quiet and comfortable environment, and living in timber frame homes is a good idea. Such houses were designed to give the occupants a high level of comfort. Such houses are also energy-efficient, and you can save much on water and electricity. Such frames are durable and can last through any condition if installed and adequately maintained. They can last you a lifetime, and you can enjoy a healthy and happy living for the rest of your life.

Timber Frame Home Constructions

Homes are built separately. In a stick-built house that you might see in a typical suburban neighborhood, two lumbers are always concealed behind drywall or plaster frame wall studs, floor joists and roof rafters, bearing home weight. In a typical log house, entire logs are piled together to shape the inner and outer walls respectively.

Large hand-hewed or milled timbers from the house frame are joined horizontally or vertically with mortise or tenon joints and beam construction. The exposed space between these large beams is sealed and protected with Structural Insulated Panels (SIPs) covering the outside of the house, and shaping the interior walls revealing the timber frame.

Timber Frame Home Advantages

Although the use of the wooden structure is widespread, not all homeowners know this style of construction. The first step in becoming a trusted construction partner is to clarify the options available to homeowners who want a rustic cabin, log house, or a timber frame home. Give time to walk through a timber frame design, so as to explain the benefits of constructing and living in a timber frame house.

This home-building strategy provides several advantages to homeowners. Example:

> ➤ Timber frame homes deliver the worlds' brightest. Such homes maintain a log home or lodge home's rustic style; however, they do provide modern conveniences that are not usually found in some log homes, such as those constructed from stacked logs.

> ➤ Timber frame homes could slash construction costs. Constructing a timber frame home can

be cheaper than building a stacked log home. Timber frame homes require less wood, as only timber frames are produced. They are also less labor-intensive to make, they save costs on labor, and needless heavy machinery such as cranes in moving building materials around the site. Usually, walls constructed from SIPs rise quickly, helping to cut time— and money — from the construction schedule.

➢ The timber frame's layout is versatile. In a few words, timber frame homes are ideal for homeowners who don't want to compromise choices. Take walls for example. Because you don't deal with stacked logs, critical components like electrical and HVAC can disappear behind them. You also need fewer partitions, as the frame protects the entire home structure. It makes room for more door and window design options and high cathedral-like ceilings. Also, because the walls are not made of solid timber, homeowners can choose to blend in and out with the building materials. You can mix indoor drywall, beadboard, log and timber trusses, exterior log siding, cedar shake, and mortar. Timber frame homes also provide dual flexibility: half-timber framing in common areas of residence (such as ample room) and half-stick framing for the majority of the house. Homeowners can then use log siding and wood paneling to create a feel throughout the entire home.

➢ Timber frame houses are eco-friendly. Trees are renewable resources, making them an eco-conscious building material. Because of timber frame homes' useless wood, it also requires fewer trees and reforestation. Moreover, most timber frame homes use organized insulated panels (SIPs) with many environmental benefits, including reduced energy consumption, less building waste, and better indoor air quality. SIPs build a well-insulated shield around a building. Homes built with SIPs regularly show 50-60% annual energy efficiency, combined with other fuel-saving strategies. (Source: Structural Panel Association)

➢ Strong timber frame houses. There's a reason to admire the timber frame homes built hundreds of years ago. Timber frame houses typically have higher fire resistance, they can withstand the impact and bend of powerful earthquake forces, and can also stand up to hurricane-or tornado-force winds, which are stronger than other forms of building.

4

PROPERTIES OF WOOD & TIMBER - PHYSICAL & CHEMICAL PROPERTIES OF WOOD

Wood is man's oldest tool for building since the stone masonry. Despite its complex natural chemical, wood has excellent properties for human use. It is readily and commercially available, conveniently machinable, manufacturable in an unlimited variety of sizes and shapes, using basic on-site building techniques. Several essential wood properties are:

> ➤ Exceptionally strong compared to weight.

> ➤ Water and electrical insulation increasingly important.

> ➤ Renewable, biodegradable asset.

Nonetheless, it also has some disadvantages that the client must be aware of. It's a "natural" material, available in limited quantities.

Physical Properties of Timber

Supporting wood characteristics make it suitable for building use are:

Specific Gravity (SG)

Typically, specific gravity (SG) and wood's main strength properties are also directly related. From the dominant structural organism, SG varies from about 0.30 to 0.90. Lower permissible model values are given to those parts with smaller growth rings (more rings per inch) and denser latewood per growth ring and lower SG.

Eco-friendly

It is one of the oldest eco-friendly construction material. Timber has low energy production, and it is a carbon absorber. Timber is a renewable material. Well reserved forests produce timber continuously, with minimal adverse effects on the soil and environmental values.

Abundant for uses

Timbers are always available. Australia has significant forest reserves, which include a plantation estate covering more than 1.6 million hectares, and the area is increasing.

Moisture Content (MC) and Shrinkage

Wood's humidity inevitably creates more problems than any other element in its use. Timber is naturally hygroscopic. It collects or releases moisture to equalize with relative humidity and atmospheric temperature. As it does, power improves. Bending strength can also increase by about 50% from green to moisture content (MC), which are found in wood members in a residential structure. Wood also shrinks as it dries, and it swells as it moisturizes with concomitant warpage potential. Fiber saturation (fsp) is crucial in this process. The stage (about 25 percent oven-dry moisture content) below which the cell's hollow-core has lost its liquid content, the cell walls begin to dry and shorten, and wood's strength starts to increase. The mechanisms of swelling and shrinkage are reversible, and they are roughly constant between fiber saturation point and 0% MC. Wood seasoning is done before production.

Thermal Properties of Wood

Wood or fungal stain does not happen if MC is below 20%. There is no practical way to prevent wood moisture change; most wood finishes and coatings slow down the process. The vapor barriers, adequate ventilation, exclusion of water from wood, or preservative treatment are essential in wood construction.

Although wood is an excellent heat conductor, its durability and other properties are adversely affected by their exposure to temperatures above 100 ° F (37,7°C) for an extended period. Combining high relative humidity and MC with high temperatures in unventilated attic areas can as well have severe effects on roofing materials and structural elements, due to the high potential for decaying species to strike. Quick remedies and caution usually prevent problems.

At temperatures above 220 ° F, wood is thermoplastic. This element, seldom found in typical construction, is an asset in producing several reconstituted board products where high temperatures and pressures are used.

Strong and lightweight

Timber is solid, durable, and efficient, making timber buildings easier and cheaper than steel or concrete. A comparison of steel and concrete reveals that, for example, radiata pine structural timber has a weight ratio of 20% more than the structural steel, and it is four to five times greater than the unreinforced packed concrete.

The possible lightweight structures in wood confer flow-on advantages with reduced foundation costs, reduced earthquake loading, and more comfortable transport. Building materials or entire structures are easy and secure to install, so deconstruction and recycle after building is a useful life.

Due to Timber's low toxicity, it needs no special safety precautions to construct with it, other than the usual dust or splinter protection. Timber frame building requires no heavy lifting equipment to make workplaces safer. Timber is non-conductive, and it has clear electrical safety advantages. New timber building has improved fire resistance due to linings that cover light frames.

Easy to install

Increasingly advanced timber frame and truss makers use high-tech prefabrication for precise and quick construction. Recyclable-Timber is an accommodating material, quickly disassembled and reworked. If a wooden building needs renovation and deconstruction, most wood-based products can be recycled and reused. Timber trusses and frames, made from sawn timber and dented metal plate connections, dominate the roof construction of small buildings, such as houses and large industrial buildings where clear spans of up to 50 meters are required. Timber trusses compete with other roof structural structures on cost, high performance, flexibility, and ready availability, backed up by the model manufacturers' design software packages to manufacturers.

Cost-effective

Comparative economic studies on different wall framing schemes show that timber frames are generally the most cost-effective solution for specific construction expenses. There are several factors to put into consideration when comparing the economies' construction values, including the complexity of the layout, site, building experience, and related building material prices. Nonetheless, comparative economic studies of different wall framing schemes demonstrate that timber frames are reliably the most cost-effective solution in terms of direct building costs.

From medium to long-term, Australian timber production projections suggest a steady, increasing demand. That means timber framing prices are likely to be more competitive for long-term homeowners. Besides, price stability is questionable for materials like steel that consume significant amounts of fossil fuels in their manufacture. Steel smelting relies heavily on the continued availability of cheap fossil fuels, a situation that is becoming highly uncertain in an increasingly energy-and security-conscious environment.

Durable

Timber qualities provide toughness. Adequate preparation, cleaning, and maintenance help to ensure life-long timber structures. Although many structures are redundant or destroyed long before the end of their natural lives, adequately designed and managed timber buildings can survive forever. The key to a long life is climate safety, freedom from insect attack, and prevention of decay through well-established model precision, surface coating schemes, choice of resilient organisms, and preservative methods. Historic timber houses adhere to these values in all countries, and Australia is no exception.

For termite-prone areas, all buildings are vulnerable to termite attacks, and protection is required, irrespective of the building materials. Protection systems depend on the physical and chemical barriers, or both, and their effectiveness depends on architecture, installation, inspection, and maintenance performance. Upon working with local building authorities, the threat of termite attack should be evaluated, and an appropriate termite management system should be introduced.

The device may include physical or chemical barriers or a termite-resistant treated lumber, or a natural termite-resistant frame may be preferred for higher-risk areas. Any management system should also include daily monitoring to ensure that the walls are not broken. Therefore, all prospective householders must know the machine form and maintenance schedule. Importantly, termites are part of Australia's ecosystem, but they can be handled successfully through education, preparation and use of cost-effective methods.

Comfortable

Well-designed timber buildings are easy living all year round, wherever you are.

Flexibility

Flexibility is one of wood's best qualities; the most sought-after is being versatile in design types and finishes. Such versatility often refers to the convenience of incorporating and altering existing buildings in order to fit changing circumstances. User-friendly functional timber gives architectural architects creative freedom to offer users with flexible choice designs. Timber is simply the best building construction material for developers, designers, and homeowners. It can also be used to create the homes they enjoy, appreciate factories and warehouses, commercial buildings, and other structures. The building timber frame approach gives architects versatility in both structure and exterior appearance. The construction incorporates high levels of thermal insulation, reducing heating costs and saving energy.

Compression Strength

An essential property of timber is that its sufficient

compression power should be used for various purposes in the construction industry.

Chemical Properties of Timber

Although it's chemically inert in relation to other products, some acids and bases influence it. Many species have proved very useful for food containers (beer cans and crates), because they are non-toxic and they give no flavor to the foods found in them. Wood systems have found frequent use to store salt and fertilizer chemicals.

5

FRAME WOOD SPECIES

When you start planning your Timber Frame project, one of the biggest questions to answer is what wood species you want to use for your frame. The wood species you choose will affect your frame size, the wood members' sizes, and other structural and engineering features. Also, determining which wood species is right for your frame and yourself is a choice that needs to be made early.

Think Function First

Before choosing which wood species to go with, think about how you want the system to function. Do you want to build a large and long warehouse that requires arches that can extend to a considerable span or a smaller storage barn? Or do you want to build a small cabin? You should also remember how the structure looks like. Talk about the big picture and what wood fits your needs.

You should also consider grain, colors, textures, and if you'd like the wood weathered or not. You have a lot of control over how the frame looks, as you think over the several combinations and choices. For example, rough-sawn oak with a golden stain would look distinctly different from weathered, chamfered Hemlock.

When dismantling the former historic timber-framed barns and shelters, it is common to find a variety of different timbers forming the architectural structure. If purpose, not beauty, was always the focus, the most likely candidates were timbers, because they're easily accessible and native to the immediate area. Accessibility is less a problem today.

We have the means to deliver timber from near or far, expanding our options list. Also, single-species timber frames are standard, though not everywhere. The options, if not determined by the intensity or length criteria, are typically based more on color, durability, and price

Wood Types

The trees that produce the wood come in two categories: deciduous and coniferous. In general, hardwood comes from deciduous trees, and softwood comes from conifer trees.

Deciduous trees are known by dropping their leaves in winter. The ash and maple fall into this category, but they are not commonly chosen as timbers for various reasons. Certain hardwoods preferred by timber framers, such as oaks and plum, are reliable and desirable, but they're hard to find in high-quality and acceptable sizes. Both hardwoods are vulnerable to dry "testing." Checking is the cracking along the timber's vertical grain as it dries. Although all wood checks to a degree, it's not uncommon for hardwood to form a check that's deep and wide enough to insert your fingertips. Checking does not necessarily affect the timber's structural integrity, especially if care is taken to preserve the heart (the center where growth rings begin) within the wood; this is called the boxed core. As a standard, to air dry one inch of timber takes around a year - so, foresee an odd "crack" in the middle of the night during the first six or eight years of loving your timber-framed home. At this time, some experimental facilities try to kiln dry timber, but, unlike the scale of wood used in furniture, timber is different in mass. The techniques are still primitive, and they may adversely affect a timber's appearance and cell structure. Since the kiln-dried appearance of fine furniture in timber cannot be expected, we opt to allowing the timber to dry up, then set in-housed joinery nicely and firmly snugged with wooden pegs.

Coniferous trees are generally evergreen. They are pine cones or needles. Douglas fir, hemlock, white and yellow oak, core pine, spruce, cedar, etc. are all suitable timber frame alternatives. They are usually prolific, test less, and emit a pleasant fragrance for years. Considered "softwoods," it shouldn't mean vulnerability. For example, Douglas fir is harvested from both sides of the Pacific Northwest Cascade mountains. It's robust, stable, and long (up to 50 feet easily), and it's readily available. It comes in various levels of quality and appearance. Light blends to hot pinks, oranges, and rusty reds. Eastern white pine, very bright in color and just as durable, is about half the price of raw material, making it a common choice. Southern pine and hemlock are on the harder end of the softwood scale, and they can be unruly and can also test like hardwoods, but they're stunning in color and texture.

We're going to look at some wood species used in Timber Framing and some that aren't used as often but are still choices to consider.

Bamboo

Bamboo is an organic material. It is technically grass, but it's usually classified as a hardwood. It's one of the earth's rare species. Bamboo grows abundantly in many parts of the world, especially in tropical and subtropical regions. The most bamboo-producing area is South Asian. Bamboo wood is pale yellow to near-gold. It is also known as the most promising building material. It has become to be popular in recent years. It's available in several forms.

Advantages of Bamboo

 ➢ Bamboos grow fast and yield high.

- Easily renewables.

- Bamboos easily mature after one or two years.

- Bamboo wood has a distinct earthy smell at play.

- Imported bamboo timber is energy-intensive, processed, and glued.

- There's the presence of tensile bamboo fibers.

- Particularly warping and moisture cupping resistant.

- Bamboo needs no nitrogen.

- It initially grows large.

- In-veneer, paper, flute, blinds, fishing rods, ladders, scaffolding, carving, etc.

Disadvantages of Bamboo

- Bamboo wood is polluting.

- Bamboo timber requires care.

- It's susceptible to infection.

- Cross-cut bamboo fibers tend to split and drag.

> Bamboo timber has confirmed skin irritation.

> Decay-fungi in bamboo wood.

> The timber quality is much higher, even above local hardwood prices.

> It's inconsistent.

Birch

Birch's a good craft-wood. It's an essential hardwood timber origin. Birch has many similar-yellow birch forms, white birch, etc. Yellow birch, also known as the black birch, is widely used. It's a vivid reddish-brown. Birch offers no natural luster.

Advantages of Birch

> Birch is the most economical.

> Aromatic outdoor birch.

> Long-lasting birch.

> Usually heavy, solid, and strong.

> Birch and glues still work efficiently, and they finish well.

> Birch is wide-ranging.

> Birch suits high-quality furniture. Birch is

long-lasting.

> Birch creates strong plywood.

> Birch is waterproof.

> Birch supports a large structure easily.

> It's utilized in bags, barrels, skateboards, furniture, and other wood pieces.

> Birch provides perfect texture.

Disadvantages of Birch

> Birch is perishable, rotting, and dying.

> Birch is vulnerable to epilepsy.

> Birch can trigger machine operation tear-outs.

> Birch is reported as "sensitizer" with respiratory irritation.

> Birch grows slowly.

> Birch is tougher than hardwoods.

Maple

Maple is one of the hardest wood species. Some of the larger maple species have valuable timber, particularly Sugar maple in North America, and

Sycamore maple in Europe. It is creamy-white and sometimes has a reddish tinge; it tends to become darker over time. Generally, it has a fine uniform texture with straight grain, but there are variations such as birdseye, tiger, flame, curly, wavy, rippled grain. Its unique color, smooth grain, and strength make maple a popular choice mainly for indoor use.

Advantages of Maple

- ➢ It is durable

- ➢ It is affordable

- ➢ Because it takes stains well, maple is often used to mimic more expensive woods

Disadvantages of Maple

- ➢ If maple is not properly sealed first, the staining can look blotchy

- ➢ It is not weather resistant

- ➢ It has a tendency to crack

Cherry

Cherry timber is grown as a tree plantation timber. Black cherry timber is also the largest of the native cherries, and it is only of commercial value. It is typical in the Eastern United Nations. In cherry timber, the grain is generally straight. It is hardwood. It has a medium-density and it's moderately durable. Also, it is used for small pieces of furniture-veneers, handles, cabinets, scientific instruments, etc.

Advantages of Cherry

> ➢ Cherry's timber is robust and strong.

> ➢ It has an elegant, uniform finish.

> ➢ It goes well, completing quickly.

> ➢ Cherry can contain pith flecks and gum pockets.

> ➢ Good workability.

> ➢ Cherries are easy to pump, nail, or stick.

> ➢ Strong bending abilities.

> ➢ It's low-stiff.

> ➢ Cherry wood is shock resistant.

> ➢ It's best used for high-end applications, including chairs, cabinet construction, boat, and musical instruments.

Disadvantages of Cherry

> ➢ It's particularly coveted.

- cherry wood is UV-sensitive.

- Cross-grain cutting.

- Cherry wood has no major size.

- When dirty, it exhibits blotchy effects.

- Cherry wood's sawdust is associated with breathing problems such as wheezing.

Mahogany

Mahogany is quality wood. It's grown commercially on almost every continent. Mahogany is widely used in furniture and cabinet-building. It's made of plywood and all sorts of trim. It shows hard grain, and it's one of the softer hardwoods commonly in use. It's an organic luster medium. Mahogany wood darkens with time, and the surface is controlled.

Advantages of Mahogany

- Mahogany is very stable.

- Termites-resistant.

- Mahogany timber tools work easily.

- Cuts computers quickly.

- Mahogany works in a simple way.

- It allows glues, paints, and finishes well.

- Bend without cracking or breaking.

- It has reasonable elastic performance.

- Mahogany timber can withstand warping for many years.

- Long-lasting, powerful, and stunning.

- It has a high density.

- Long bits of wood.

- Mahogany is for-veneers, musical instruments, carving, etc.

Disadvantages of Mahogany

- Wood is susceptible to pests.

- It drops and drops during machining.

- It is recorded as a "sensitizer."

- As mahogany wood comes into contact with air, heavy mahogany color emerges.

- Slight dulling can occur in this timber.

- Mahogany timber causes respiratory issues, eye pain, burning blood, vomiting, dizziness, asthma-type symptoms, etc.

Oak

Oak's a gorgeous hardwood. For thousands of years, it has been used as timber. It's a grained flat. It is mostly employed for light construction, such as homeware, wine barrels, firewood, etc. It's less costly than Douglas fir. Hardwoods usually aren't as stable as softwoods, so they prefer to twist and test more. Oak, in particular, is subjected to surface checks–when a timber gets several small splits & cracks just on its surface. Heart checks also prevail in oak. Some of our customers like the oak being indigenous to our area, and the wood doesn't have to go so far to finish up our building. There are various oak types: green, black, mixed. White oak is weatherproof, and red oak is a little redder than white oak. Mixed is just as it looks, a red-white mix. Buying mixed-oak saves time and money.

Advantages of Oak

➢ The timber of oak is extremely strong.

➢ It's long-lasting.

➢ It's a long-lived thing.

➢ It's used for cladding.

- Oakwood is fungal-resistant.

- It's great for glues, nails, and screws.

- The weight is lighter.

- Oakwood is resistant to decline.

- Oakwood is highly resistant to the use of preservatives.

- Hand tools can be used.

Disadvantages of Oak

- Oak timber drawbacks are high.

- It's difficult to use.

- It is low in humidity.

- Oakwood is unsafe for outdoor use.

- The acid content of oak wood is challenging to treat.

- The iron galvanized or copper nails of the oak timber respond.

Cedar

Cedar is a high-quality softwood that comes from various trees known as cedars. Where exposed wood beams' strength and beauty are significant, cedar is the only salvation and perfect fit for this. It is employed in the design of four-landscape, park, greenhouse, etc. It is different, due to its medium strength and softness. The advantage of Cedar is natural, and it's effectively a workable material.

Cedar is white and red, of course. It can be painted with natural oil or black color, depending on the owner's choice. Naturally, when exposed to nature, cedar is rich in oils that preserve the wood, making it perfect for outdoor use. Cedar timber is naturally resistant to rot and insects, making it extremely tough and durable.

Western red cedar is a premium slow-growing timber, harvested on British Columbia's northern coast. This magnificent, tight-grained wood is one of the most deteriorating and insect-resistant softwoods. When you live in extreme weather conditions, western red cedar may be your perfect choice.

Western red cedar logs are known for their flared ends, bringing dimension and elegance to timber structures, making it one of our customers' favorites. Yellow Cedar is another prominent timber type which is widely used for canoe paddles.

Advantages of Cedar

> It is weather-resistant.

- Cedar gives a natural wood look.

- It is light in weight.

- It works easily.

- It is dimensionally stable.

- It has long-time durability.

- Remarkable resistance to insects and decay.

- Smooth to touch.

- High quality of consistency.

- It exhibits fairly prominent growth.

- It shows high resistance to warping and twisting.

- It helps to reduce noise in specific areas.

- It is sustainable.

- It is utilized by in-cladding, decking, roofing, and fencing.

Disadvantages of Cedar

- Cedar dust may be an irritant.

- It has low strength.

> It can cause splintering during some operations.

Pine

Pine is a popular softwood choice for many construction projects. It is inexpensive and readily available, ranges from clear to knotty. As it comes from plantations, it is a renewable resource. White pine is particularly good for timber framing. It is a stable tree. It has good straight grain, can be easily painted, planes well, and is a high hand hewing wood.

Advantages of Pine

> It is cheaper than hardwood

> It doesn't require reinforcements

> Lightweight

> It resists shrinking and swelling

> Good elasticity

> It has attractive grain options.

Disadvantages of Pine

> Common lumber often has defects

- It often features knots and knotholes

- It is susceptible to Scratches and Dents

- It can be easily damaged

Walnut

Walnut is wood with premium quality. It's a hardwood expert. While the grain is flat, it may be irregular. Walnut wood is genuinely beautiful, brings a great deal in interior design, and it has a mild luster of light. Walnut wood is of medium toughness; it has a standard size.

Advantages of Walnut

- Walnut brings the grain a vibrant focus.

- Automated and hand tools work well.

- Walnut wood is an excellent tool to transform and carve.

- It is possible to make the best glues and polishes in walnut wood.

- Walnut wood reacts well to the bending of air.

- It has good stability in its dimensions.

- It's immune to shock.

> The texture is perfect.

> The overall strength of the walnut is great.

> It is weak in rigidity.

Disadvantages of Walnut

> Walnut is tough.

> As a "sensitizer," it was published.

> It causes inflammation of the eyes and skin.

> Walnut wood is high in domestic species prices.

> It has a process of reasonable care.

> Walnut wood has trouble containing acid content.

> Walnut timber has a thickness problem.

> It's not immune to termite.

> It's difficult.

Fir

Fir is one of the best-known species of wood in the world. For a wide range of applications, it is a leading building product. It's a species of softwood. Fir has a very flat seed, and it has become the traditional timber framing woods of choice. Tin-housing, frame, flooring, fascia lining, bargeboards, and pergolas are the uses of fir timber. It is one of North America's most common wood types. The hue varies from light-red to pale-yellow. Douglas fir was a long-time engineering favorite. Douglas fir is one of the best softwoods available, making it ideal for timber frames and traditional log houses. Douglas fir has a red and a white wood logo. Douglas Fir is free of heart centers, meaning that the typical "bull's eye" heartwood located in the middle of most timbers is missing. Heart-free timber is less susceptible to inspection and more durable than Heartwood timber.

Advantages of Fir

➢ Color variations occur in Fir woods.

➢ Machines work for firing and turning well.

➢ Fir is relatively long-lasting.

➢ It's amazing.

➢ It is resistant to a decline in moderation.

➢ Firwood has a low resistance to shock.

➢ It's got good power.

➢ The standard procedure allows fir to be joined

satisfactorily.

Disadvantages of Fir

- ➤ It lacks tensile strength.

- ➤ It's very tough to treat.

- ➤ fir hand-hewn

- ➤ continues to peel and doesn't look the best when you try to create the finish with Douglas fir.

- ➤ The fir wood is very solid.

Cypress

Cypress trees are conifers, but unlike other softwoods, they shed foliage in fall like hardwoods. Although Cypress is a softwood, it is grouped and manufactured with hardwoods. Cypress trees usually grow in a wet climate, with a distinctive look and smell once cut. Younger Cypress trees are relatively robust, stable, and strong, resistant to deterioration, making them perfect for indoor and outdoor use. The wood retains organic preservative oils for quite a very long time. Cypress carries suitable resins and glues. It also flies well. It's less common than Douglas fir, and it's equivalent to Oak. The cypress siding that was used on houses in the 1700s has held up so well that it is sometimes removed when these structures are no longer functional and used again in modern home construction projects.

Advantages of Cypress

- ➤ It has a water repellent nature

- ➤ Cypress wood is very durable

- ➤ It stands very well to the weather

- ➤ Thanks to its organic oil, called cypressene, there is no need to apply chemical protective treatments

Disadvantages of Cypress

- ➤ It tends to fade over time

- ➤ It needs the periodical application of a sealant, to protect the siding from warping or cracking

Hemlock

Hemlock is produced from Tsuga, which is a genus of conifers. It is a highly economical softwood for farmhouses and barns. It tends to be honey and it is uniformly colored. It is readily both for machining and handling with hand tools.

Some hemlock stands may have a defect called

shake. The shake is delamination of wood growth rings. Nevertheless, shake also happens after a timber frame has been up for about a year. Shake in timber frames is not a structural problem. The engineer's designer frames can compensate for a shake, test, and other wood motions over time. Shake in hemlock is typically not a structural issue, but it can make a post & beam frame look rustic. Cost may vary by grade. Costly hemlock lumber has extensively processed to condition them for work. Less expensive hemlock lumber tends to be rough cut and less processed.

Advantages of Hemlock

➤ It is sturdy, has long-grain

➤ It is renewable

➤ It is rotting resistant

➤ The low resin level allows this wood to take very well paints and stains

Disadvantages of Hemlock

➤ It is not a very good weather-resistant wood

➤ It doesn't handle pests infestation well

➤ Hemlock lumber sometimes requires a slow

curing time to be suitable for some projects

Reclaimed

Reclaimed Timber is wood regained from old buildings, including barns, mills, warehouses, and other structures. People love reclaimed wood, because it's recycled, making it a green building material, and because it looks very different. Since reclaimed wood is usually old-growth lumber, mostly 100 years old or more, it has a lovely dense grain that can be revealed when resawing parts. It also has a lot of rustic and antique quality when used. When buying antique wood, we designate either "hand-hewn" timber or "resawn" timber. A band saw to our requirements can cut the resawn timber. The hand-hewn wood comes to us as it is, and we write it in a timber frame. Reclaimed timber frames are lovely, very rare, and also very costly.

Advantages of Reclaimed

- ➢ It is suitable for multiple uses

- ➢ Ecologically friendly

Disadvantages of Reclaimed

- ➢ It is subject to be infested by pests: it should be kiln-dried to ensure invasive pests are killed

> It requires an extensive inspection: if it is not purchased from a company that sorts and processes it, reclaimed wood may hide dangers like nails.

Glued Laminated Timber

Glued timber is obtained by gluing a special composition of well-dried wood in three layers. Glulam beams are composed of small sections of wood which are cut into strips and then nailed or laminated together, creating a robust and durable wood material that can be used to extend over large stretches. It is distinct from cross-laminated timber, a product in which every layer of boards is usually oriented perpendicular to adjacent layers and glued on the wide faces of each board. Only carefully selected raw materials are used, such as Siberian pine or cedar, larch, and ale. It is a good option for clients to stop natural timber searches, shakes or other natural variations or inconsistencies. It's also a great choice for those searching for long and elegant rounded beams.

Advantages of Glued Laminated

> Its structure eliminates the drying-up of wood

> It is very easy to assemble

> High level of protection from decay, fungus, and insects

> It has excellent thermal insulation properties

Disadvantages of Glued Laminated

> Due to its process of composition, it is expensive

Plywood

Plywood is a very handy building material manufactured by layering off thin sheets of wood veneer. It can be cut in any shape. It is cost-effective when used in structural applications such as plywood flooring, walls, partitions, formwork, etc. because of its high strength and stability.

Advantages of Plywood

> It has high strength and stability

> It has water and chemical resistance

> It has flexibility or bendability

> It has fire resistance

> Sound and thermal insulation

Disadvantages of Plywood

> Because the layers of veneers are seen at the edges, edges have to be finished either with laminate or veneer

➤ It often gets a splinter from the edges during transportation.

6

TIMBER FRAME HOUSE DESIGN

You can imagine a large, timber-accented manor or a little cabin or a cottage during the daydreaming of your perfect dream home. The dramatic rustic shapes, the sense of eternal resilience, and the appeal of nature all draw you to this unique vision of your private sanctuary. Your idea can truly become real, but you need to understand the basics of what this dream house means. Timber frame houses are the pinnacle of longevity and open space, but as they are in many respects, not traditional building homes, it helps to spend as much time thinking about the design that can become your family home for as many decades as possible.

A timber frame house is a big wood celebration. Great posts rise from the ground and are attached overhead with glove-like precision in a growing network of columns, rafters, and braces. Then, the whole system— which can last for decades— stands uncovered as a proof of the skill of the craftsman. It's like bringing the vastness of the outside indoors. Today, timber frame construction is a relatively high-end option. It helps homebuilders to make something more unique from 2 x 4s and other dimensional timber, than traditional frame construction.

Anatomy of a Timber Frame

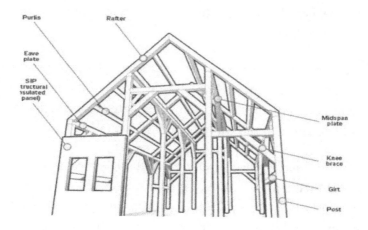

The timber frame's difference comes from significant wooden components connected to a cathedral-like frame that needs no internal load-bearing wall. The posts and rafters are joined together by girts, plates, and purlins, while diagonal knee braces provide stability. Factory-built insulated structural panels (SIPs) are housing all in one roof, wall, insulation, and window.

How a timber frame company works

Usually, a timber-frame company, an assembly line of posts and beams awaits the final details before the delivery and installation on-site. While each part is sliced to exact size and joints are formed on machines for computer numerical control (CNC), most things are more comfortably done in an old-fashioned way— with a labyrinth and chisel. One designer has developed a catalog of components with hundreds of pre-designed features, allowing homeowners to receive a near-custom design.

The parts were assembled to ensure that everything matches, then the whole frame of a house will be removed and shipped to the home site, along with the wall-forming structural isolated panels (SIPs).

The typical house goes up at quick speed once the components arrive, most times in just a few days. Yet, particularly, timber framing costs more than stick framing, with prices ranging from $150 to $325 per square foot— or at least, $375,000 per square foot.

The added price is worth it for an increasing number of homeowners. Timber framing has intrinsic power and elegance when you find beauty in the joinery and how the elements are fitted together.

The Factory

Features like stopped bevels and chamfers enhance a traditional timber-frame home's handcrafted feel.

The Job Site

Workers build a frame from on-site factory-shaped

timbers. Mortise-and-tenon joints are typically sealed with wooden pegs— by drilling holes and pressing the pegs in — while using distinctly modern instruments: a heavy-duty electric drill and a dead-blow mallet. Precise machining has produced joints just 132 inches (3,3m). That slips typically with a soft clicking. If required, a ratchet puller, commonly called a come-along, brings larger pieces together.

The Frame

In the past, barn raisings were a community event — mostly because the assembly floor needed many people, and animals of many people, to raise the large boxes, often called the bents. Today, a hydraulic crane lifts each frame as workers softly lead the construction.

Nowadays, it is possible to bring 40 to 50 prefab sub-assemblies together on a construction site, instead of 40,000 to 50,000 individual pieces. It's not only simpler but also much better. Straight tenons lock up as they fall onto vertically bored mortises.

The Roof

Larger timber-frame roofs are made of rafters, each lifted in place and placed on the plates. In some instances, horizontal purlins attach wide-spaced rafters. The crew meets the prefabricated roof elements on the floor in this building, and proceed to call in the crane to raise the assembly. A groove (below) slips onto a vertical tongue in the paper. When the frame is pulled together, the connecting girt fits securely in the post-house.

A House With No Nails

Long-time ago, framers put lumber between timbers to carry indoor lath and plaster, and outdoor cladding such as clapboard. Structural insulated panels (SIPs) are up to 612 inches(15m), thick with 3.7-7 inches (9,3 to17 cm)R-values. Each board has an interior and exterior foam base.

The Completed Timber-Frame Home

Like traditional studs and joists, a timber frame is a sculptural feature of interior designs.

What Are The Best Logs For Building My Log Home?

The log types for building your log home are significant. The right selection will determine your project's cost, and choosing the right timber for your home will as well ensure a sound structure that can withstand the elements.

Selecting the Right Timber

Relatively high trees match house logs; they grow slowly with near growth rings. Dense wood creates close growth rings, resulting in less splitting and testing as the log dries. You can see how close a tree's rings are by looking up, or at the cross-section of a cut log. Each triangular line or circle reflects one year of tree life growth.

One of the most critical components of choosing trees is to ensure that, when the sap level is low, they fall in winter. It eliminates testing and sap stain (mold) risks. This is an essential factor in choosing the best logs for your house.

In the previous "Wood Types" section of this book, there is an overview of the most common kinds of timber that can be suitable for your project.

Kiln Drying Timber

You may see an option to buy kiln-dried Douglas Fir wood. Based on the system you are creating, you may want the wood kiln dried. Kiln drying is a method used to dry the wood very slowly so that it does not harm the wood. One of the most significant benefits for kiln-dried timbers is that wood is smooth and secure, and it's also ideal for showcasing timber frame construction. You often see dried timber in old churches.

7

TIMBER TOOLS

It makes the work more fun and reliable, whether you are new to timber framing or a seasoned expert with the right tool for the job. Timber framing comes with its distinct set of tools, like other companies. Some of the resources you may already have, but when you look at an 8x10, you may need something a little larger than what you're using. While you don't need to go out and spend a lot to get the necessities, be confident. You can create your collection after learning what you need.

What materials are you using as a framer of wood? It is possible to divide them into four different sections. Chisels are the first. The second will be shipped. Then, it is time to think about methods for measuring and tagging. Some other resources that you need to use are also blended in here.

The timber framing world comes with its own particular set of tools, like any art. And if you're new to this kind of job, having the right timber framing equipment in your kit is critical. Luckily, to outfit yourself with the necessities, it doesn't have to cost a little fortune. Of course, once you get more into this sort of thing, you will always discover something else you probably think you want. Nonetheless, you can get by with a relatively small handful for a robust starter set.

Below are lists of essential tools for timber framing, showcasing both cheap options for beginners and more excellent choices for someone who can stick with this line of work.

The Essential Timber Framing Tools

I'm not going to bother you with stuff like tape dimensions, pencils, etc. that should ideally be apparent here. The list includes tools that you don't own if you are not already building timber. I also don't include things like rigging equipment and the like this is purely a list of designs and cutting wood pieces that are definitely required.

Framing Square

A framing square is a tool that will pave the way for everything else to follow. It's significant for architecture, and you can use it to measure roof angles and all kinds of fun things if you know your stuff. There is no doubt that you need a square for square rule timber framing. Perhaps, two of them.

Low-cost option: Vintage at the flea market, luckily,

you can find vintage squares fairly available at flea markets, and many of them are not in terrible shape either. Nonetheless, be sure that the square is indeed square. How are you going to check? Use the 3-4-5 law to calculate between the 12″ (30cm) and 16″ (40cm) gradations on both legs with a tape measure. It ought to spell 20″(50cm). Put it back if it's anything that. Don't waste more than a few bucks on an old square, and remember— light rust can easily be removed at all times.

Costly Option: Timber Frame HQ Design Tool, Standard Square Chappell, Borneman Layout System.

You may want to "move" to something more than a regular framing square once you have completed a frame, two or three. Sold through the Timber Framers Guild company, the Borneman design tool is really handy. Consider it as a speed square designed explicitly for timber framing. Precise and quick laying out of mortises and tenons is easily achieved with this device. It's almost like lying.

The Chappell Universal Square (or "the best square in the universe" as they say) is a pretty fancy square with precise gradations and nifty tables of calculation. I can't claim to be "the best" directly, so you'll have to find out for yourself.

Combination Square

A mix square is a convenient little device to be next to. It's not the first and foremost design tool, but it's a lovely thing to have around you for different calculations and marking tasks. You can easily pass dimensions, and they are as well outstanding in mortise to test depths and square.

Low-cost option: Vintage, or Empire 6"(15), 7"(17cm) and Stanley 12"(30cm) square Vintage combination squares aren't too hard to find as well, but it's less comfortable to locate one that's easy to read, doesn't rock in its route and has smooth motion. Nonetheless, they're out there. If you don't want to hunt, Empire should make a decent square of 6"(15cm) and 7"(17cm). (I like the 7" — the extra inch is often beneficial.) Stanley also makes an excellent hybrid square size of 12"(30cm).

Expensive option: Brand new Starrett combination square, Starrett combo squares of any length are the cream o' the crop. These are cast iron which is manufactured in the United States; they're smooth as butter and easy to read. They're a pretty penny, though one is the same quality as six and lower-cost equipment. Even if those who use them swear by them. Also, if you're going to use it on a weekly or very regular basis, it's all fine and good.

Hand Saw

Sawing choices can be very personal, and people can

be quite specific about what they like, whether it's a Western-style saw that cuts on the push or a Japanese saw that cuts on the pull stroke. Any type you pick, if you go on the hand tool route, an above-average saw is a must-have.

Low-cost option: Stanley Sharptooth 20"(50cm) saw Stanley make a decent "Sharptooth" saw. The 20"(50cm) model with 9 points per inch is a respectable choice for people who are familiar with Western-style saws, slicing on the push stroke. You can easily find them for about $30 in your local hardware store. They can't be re-sharpened quickly (if at all), but they're perfect. I got tired of them myself and started to favor other saws, but for an introductory/budget saw, they're not all that bad.

Expensive option: GyokuchoRyoba Saw 11" (300 mm), Z-SAW 333, any similar folding Silky saw I'd like to see must be a Japanese-style saw that cuts the pull stroke, and there are several options. Perhaps, the most important thing to consider is the size of the blade — get at least 11" (300 mm) of something. A ryoba is the right choice because on the same handle; you get two blades in one — a crosscut and a rip saw. A good blade of ryoba should not be more costly than a reasonable western saw. Silky makes any number of folding saws on the worksite that is handy, and the longer blade lengths get a pretty amount. It's your decision. Try a few before you buy, if you can. I understand that's not always possible, but on a coarse-toothed Japanese crosscut saw, you don't have a lot to spare.

Framing Chisel

Framing chisels are, of course, one of the most flexible cutting tools for joinery, other than a saw. Everybody needs at least one knife, good for wasting tenons, slicing mortises, or paring joints. In the usability category, a 1 1/2"(2 to 3cm) chisel is hard to beat — it will slice (almost) any joint you'll ever need to sever. It is also small enough not to weigh you down. There are less flexible two-inch chisels— the same for 1″ chisels. These may potentially be good to have, but consider your first goal which is 1 1/2"(2 to 3 cm).

Low-cost option: 1 1/2"(2 to 3 cm) is an antique chisel, I'm going, being honest. Sadly, I can count on one hand the amount of framing chisels I saw for sale on the flea markets. So, I bought nearly every one of them worth a lick o' sugar. Why were they so mysterious to me, I'm not sure, but they were. Maybe in your area, you're going to have better luck— it might be a regional thing.

An important note: the backside of the tool may be the most critical thing to consider when buying a used chisel. It should be dead flat, or at least, as close as possible. (When searching for old tools, sometimes, hold a straight edge to test for flatness.) Why? One of the most boring things I can think about is flattening the back of the chisel, and without a flat back, the device will never live up to its full (sharp) potential. I'm not going to go on too much here (maybe in another post), so, please make sure you buy one that is as flat as possible. Bevels can always be context, but lapping a chisel's back makes it much harder to bring it to the dead surface. It can be completed, but routine labor can take several hours.

As a general, I hate buying online used devices, but if I like the dealer, I will accept it. Patrick Leach, Hyperkitten, and Jim Bode are good choices, and they have decent framing chisels from time to time, but they are not always a deal.

Expensive option: Barr 1 1/2"(2 to 3 cm) chisel and Robert Sorby 1 1/2" (2 to 3 cm) chisel Barr Tools is the go-to for new chisels. That's because in this day and age, at least in the USA, Barr Quarton is one of the few individuals who hand-forge value framing chisels. These are fantastic devices of the highest quality, ready to use when they arrive in the mail. The backs are dead flat, and the angles are completely sharpened. It's not a cheap buy at $130+, but if you think you could spend $50 on a decent vintage chisel, plus potentially several hours getting it in useable condition... well, after all, $130 might not look so bad. Besides, you can endorse an artisan of top-notch. There are also the painting chisels of Robert Sorby, which are significantly less expensive than chisels of Barr. The color is not as good as it is, but it is going to do the same job.

Mallet

A mallet is a method for grunting. They were designed to hit chisels and other similar devices. Mallets are ideal for framing of timber and making sure it is in the 32 oz(907 gr). Give or take the unit. They should be heavy enough to be successful in their mission, but not so heavy that after swinging one all day, the wrists are on the brink of destruction.

Low-Cost option: Happily, making your mallet is a pretty simple affair; DIY turned or carved mallet. It doesn't matter what it looks like as long as it's secure and appropriately weighted. It's up to you (and the tools you have access to) whether you want to carve it or turn it on. Your choice of wood should be thick and not susceptible to breaking— other good options are hickory, dogwood, and Osage. When the wood is raw, a mallet will be more comfortable to make, but once adequately polished, they excel in use.

Expensive option: Wood is a great polyurethane hammer or Garland split head rawhide hammers. If you want a durable, ready-to-go stick, you have a few options. The plastic head mallet, somewhat ironically called 'Wood is Great', is more or less unbreakable. Some may like this because the poly head absorbs some of the impact shocks. The Garland split-head rawhide mallet, often designed as a tank and with replaceable rawhide hammerheads, is more hammer-like in its operation. These are perfectly weighed and have a good hit.

Block Plane

Of all the aircraft that you may want or need while doing timber frame joinery, a block plane is one of the handy tools for daily use. A block plane can shave end grain and also repair convex end cuts or knees. They are suitable for tight fit tuning in tenons, and are perfect for chamfering edges. We even render rough-sawn wood for a decent eraser. Also, it is flexible.

Low-cost option: Vintage Stanley #60 1/2, or any other good condition block plane. My first choice would be a low angle block plane like Stanley #60 1/2, which is providing all the usual block plane capability, but it's just better. The extra low angle means that they can be more effective in working with weird or complicated wheat. A regular angle block plane is also excellent, and the flea markets are more popular. People have written volumes on aircraft, so I'll say — find one that fits well with your hand, can be brought to work without too much fuss, and will also not cost you a bundle. Recall that straight edge to make sure the plane's sole is flat.

Expensive Option: All modern, Lie-Nielsen, or Veritas Block Plane. If you want a genius piece of metal in the shape of a block plane, there are several companies ready to receive your wallet's full content. Veritas and Lie-Nielsen are developing a perplexing number of new planes, including several block plane types. I don't see any reason to look for a $300 plane for timber framing when you can get a $10-$30 antique machine. Nonetheless, I promised a "costly option," so, you're going there!

Drilling Tools

It's a tough class. The drilling choices are quite small in the domain of the hand tool. That's because timber framing needs some pretty giant holes (1-2"/ 2-5cm) for hog mortises, and peg holes to dig. For anything in the 1" range, a brace orbit is perfect (mostly just drilling peg holes), but you will need a severe auger to drill mortises. With these materials, it's tough to rely solely on t-handle augers to dig. Frankly, it's pretty hard to use. Yet, if you can spot one in good shape, they pay almost nothing on the flea markets.

Low-cost option: The most common diameter hole sizes for joinery are 1"(2cm), 1 1/2"(3,8cm) and 2"(5cm) t-handles. The most common depth of hole sizes for joinery are 1"(2cm), 1 1/2"(3,8cm) or 2"(5cm). So, you're going to need to be able to drill specific measurements. You'll also need some strong elbow grease as well. Better still.

Expensive option: A wood-framed boring machine with 1"(2cm), 1 1/2"(3,8cm), and 2"(5cm) drill bits. It is an excellent investment, providing the top pick for any serious timber frame building drilling job. All the wood-framed boring machines so far are vintage by definition (no one was made in at least 60, 70 + years). Also, there are several different models out there: Millers Falls, Ajax, Boss, James Swann, and so on.

The Millers Falls is considered the "Cadillac" of the dull machines. It is spectacularly built, incredibly made, and sturdy, and it has some nifty features including a robust depth stop, and a simple gear reversal shift (to quickly get the bit out of the holes). These are excellent tools that are powerful. You can find one if you're lucky without spending an arm or leg on the craigslist. Nonetheless, you must keep an eye on it.

Sharpening Kit

For anyone dealing with edge materials, a sharpening kit is essential. (Don't think just because I'm listing it as the last product, that it's any less important than the others!) There are several sharpening alternatives out there, and I'm just going to forget my "cheap" and "costly" options and mention a few different possibilities. All have distinct advantages and disadvantages.

Choices vary from a glass plate (or plain granite) sandpaper to Waterstones, gemstones, oil rocks, and others. Sandpaper and glass are inexpensive, but daily sandpaper must be obtained, and it can wear out easily. Coarse grits are good to describe an angle and also lap the back of a chisel.

Japanese Waterstones slice very quickly, but they must be maintained periodically. Working with them is a bit messy. If you have a collection of Waterstones, you might want to flatten the stones with a super rough diamond chip. Also, diamond stones they don't need to be preserved, but they can be very costly. These also have a "look", which is distinct from Waterstones. It is also highly recommended for the finishing touch to keep a leather strop with honing compound around, regardless of which system you choose.

Bonus Tools

Although they are undoubtedly useful, the following timber framing devices are not strictly necessary. Without these, you can get by, but in some cases, they give you some distinct advantages. None of these are tools that are strictly for beginners.

Slick — Imagine a large chisel on a long handle, about 2–3″ (5-7 cm)high. These are meant for paring joints, such as tenon cheeks and deep mortises. They work well to define a beautiful flat surface.

Chisel — A corner chisel will help speed up the scraping of the mortise. The corners are often the trickiest part of cleaning a mortise, and a well-sharpened corner chisel will help to accelerate things along. They are a little challenging to manage and very precise, but in good working order, a corner chisel can help save time and effort.

Axe — This is one of the favorite tools to use. For wasting tenon material, they can be used to great advantage, and even for paring the tenon close to its final size. You can also cut down on cuts with a professional eye. There is an impressive range of axes in the world. Nonetheless, an excellent scale to have around would be something a little bigger than the "typical" camp axis (with a handle around 19"/48cm and a head weighing around 2 lbs-0,9 kg.). My preference axis is the GransforsBruks Hunters Axis — it's incredibly well-balanced, can swing with one or two arms, and the metal value is very high. A vintage Kent side hatchet pattern is also a good one to look for in the flea markets.

To get you started, this should be more than enough!

8

TIMBER CONSTRUCTION IN TERMS OF ECO-FRIENDLINESS

In early 2017, the German Masonry and Housing Construction Association (Deutsche Gesellschaft für Mauerwerks-und Wohnungsbau e. V., or DGfM for short) made a book. It states that "The ecological impact of houses built using traditional cement frame, brick, and block work methods are equivalent to the timber frame buildings, estimating a useful life of 50 to 80 years." It also reported that timber houses are more expensive to build, according to comprehensive sustainability analysis.

Currently, timber construction methods account for about 15% of all new detached, semi-detached and duplex houses built in Germany—and their share is increasing. Over the years, German self-builders' attitudes have changed. Sustainable and environmentally friendly fabrics are becoming increasingly popular, likewise those that are conducive to a healthy living environment. The masonry lobby is therefore understandably worried, and it tries to protect its portion of the building market, although it is still the lion share at 75 percent. It could justify why the DGfM commissioned three reports from Darmstadt's Polytechnic University. It seemed to have hoped to slow down the timber construction industry's growth.

Turning Resources into Useful Materials

No other raw material gives rise to such a wide range of products as wood. In terms of lightweight and versatility, it is timelessly stunning and compelling. It breathes and also regulates moisture, and it is possible to reuse even the smallest bits of scrap and waste from its production. Wood then satisfies the pressing need for a sustainable economic model to conserve and also reuse resources to the greatest extent possible. It is a green building material that is ecologically sustainable, and it maps the course into the future. It is important to remember that eco-friendly construction covers all aspects of the lifecycle of a building: from planning and constructing to use and restoration, and all the way to demolition and disposal.

The frugal use of electricity and natural resources while mitigating harm to the environment is essential at all times. Consequently, all its plants adhered to these extremely stringent sustainability standards that were established.

Product Life Cycles

It all begins with wood, a natural raw material produced in the forest. Based on the record of the

German Prefabricated Building Association (Bundesverband Deutscher Fertigbau), enough new wood grows in Germany every 23 seconds to build a whole single-family home. Wood is the only renewable resource that connects and also absorbs toxic carbon dioxide from the atmosphere, making it an outstanding environmental footprint. A cubic meter of wood absorbs about a ton of carbon from the environment–which is not emitted again until the completion of the material life cycle, for example, burning it to create heat. The critical point here is that no more CO_2 than the initially released one was introduced to the air even then.

It ensures that timber and imported wood have an outstanding ecological footprint, among other things. So, we're talking about a completely renewable building material.

Reduction and Storage of CO2

Forests are a potential carbon sink, and in Germany's forests alone, about 1.2 billion tons of coal are being sequestered. A hectare of forest absorbs about 13 tons of CO_2 every year by removing it from the atmosphere through the normal photosynthesis cycle. Each molecule of carbon dioxide consists of a carbon atom and two atoms of oxygen. In a simple way, light energy is used to pry each molecule apart, hold the "poor" carbon atom by inserting it into organic compounds, then release one of the two "strong" atoms of oxygen. The coal is then naturally deposited in the tissues of plants.

These types of wood-based materials–glulam, OSB, particleboard, solid wood, and so on, used for building houses, making furniture, producing parquet and laminate flooring–thus also contain carbon once removed from the air. Therefore, it makes sense from the point of view of what is best for the world to be capable of providing as much energy as possible in buildings for as long as possible. It helps to prevent adverse climate change.

As a result, when we use wood to create new buildings or to renovate existing ones, add annexes and additional frames, and then render floors and furniture, the coal found in them is retained throughout the entire life cycle of the items.

Every cubic meter of wood supplemented by other building materials, on average, reduces the amount of free CO_2 in the air by one ton.

Construction Times and Costs of Different Materials

A study claims that masonry is just as environmentally friendly as timber and that it is also more expensive to build a house with stone.

Scientists at ARGE I Kiel have calculated that it costs more than four times less on average to build a new single-family stone house than a comparable timber home.

It's a fact that timber construction materials are cheaper. Performance has its cost, and more self-builders keep paying for it. Yet, taking these factors into consideration in the design, construction and living processes of a home, it pays off with the slightly higher significant investment.

Timber frame construction is a predominantly dry method in which a structure can be raised from prefabricated materials and also sealed against the weather in just a few days, unlike masonry or concrete frame approaches. Extensive prefabrication allows vulnerabilities such as joints, connections between different material types, stagnant moisture, and long building times to be routinely avoided. Furthermore, no additional space is needed to store building materials, as the prefabricated modules can be delivered straight to the building site on time, and installed there immediately.

The emphasis here is about the time that can be saved in comparison with conventional building techniques. The fast pace of building decreases spending on follow-up works, and the house can also be rented sooner, enabling buyers to avoid paying rent while waiting for the completion of their new home. Yet, wood has another significant advantage: It is solid, given its much lower weight, and it can be used as joists, boards, and panels. An existing structure can also be expanded horizontally by installing up to six additional floors on top of the roof. For densely settled urban areas where few empty lots are open for construction, this is particularly attractive.

Energy Efficiency: the Right Insulation Material

It is also beneficial for insulating, in addition to the physical advantages of wood. It is possible to build alternative energy-efficient solutions such as zero energy and passive houses, using timber frame, cement, blockwork, and concrete frame technology. Nonetheless, those who use traditional methods rarely bother to use ecological separation materials. Masonry is usually mixed with ingredients that are of very low-cost, but environmentally harmful, such as elastic concrete, calcium silicate, perlite, foam glass, and mineral fiber. It can save time in the short term, but it is far from being weather-sensitive to make and also store these items. The timber frame construction uses sustainable insulation materials such as flax, silk, wood fiber, wood wool, and cellulose. Some firms also provide monetary incentives to encourage their use.

The report also concentrated on the latter, condemning the trend of "binding" owners arbitrarily to relying on renewable energy sources.

It argues that while heat pumps, solar heating, exhaust air heat recovery in ventilation systems, etc. may increase energy efficiency, and these technologies incur unacceptably high costs for owners who are unable to take advantage of government's support. Therefore, it calls on the German state's government to also subsidize concrete and masonry construction projects (which are just as environmentally friendly), so as to make these approaches more desirable.

Living Space and Healthy Living

Wood is a healthy life! And we're happy to explain why. In addition to the several benefits of building with wood-quicker construction and the will of self-builders to do much of the interior finishing work themselves if they wish, buildings can also be changed quickly and flexibly when their needs change. Besides, wood and engineered wood are incredibly healthy, low-emission materials that make people with allergies breathe easily. The important thing is that consumers look carefully and choose licensed goods of high quality. Wood products are extremely environmentally friendly and safe, because they do not contain harmful binders, but the wood they produce comes from sustainable domestic forests.

Besides being extremely artistic, wood offers warm and healthy living spaces. Wood has always had a substantial impact on people; it is considered warm and comfortable. Improving the buildings' indoor environment has been shown, and unlike other building materials, there is even a proven antibacterial effect that can help alleviate health problems.

Special attention should be given to sustainability and eco-friendliness, and the positive impact of wood on the indoor environment. It offers a very nice "bio climate" that significantly increases the inhabitants' health and well-being. In partnership with the Austrian Human Research Institute, a study conducted by Holzcluster Steiermark found that children learn faster, have a lower pulse rate, and also feel better in wood-containing classrooms.

Wood also has some regulating moisture properties: It absorbs moisture from the ambient air and pass it out when it reduces relative humidity. Open-pored wood can even clean the air by removing pollutants, thus, further improving the indoor environment. Nevertheless, one quality of wood is that it cannot be treated electrostatically, therefore, it does not produce particles, making it particularly suitable for people with allergies. Wood is an all-encompassing material (no pun intended!) in terms of look and sound, antistatic quality, scent, natural moisture control, and much more.

Even if all these advantages don't inspire you, at

least, you can look forward to a more spacious timber frame building home. Exterior walls can also be significantly thinner than conventional building systems, such as concrete frame and masonry, resulting in 10% additional floor space without compromising energy efficiency.

Fire Protection

The masonry building industry loves branding with the message, "Stone is not burning!" Although many insurers look at stone and wood in the same manner, it also likes to claim that residential insurance costs more when constructed with a rock. It is widely believed, albeit incorrectly, that a higher number of traditional buildings were burning wooden houses. Interior surfaces, chairs, etc. continue to burn before the whole building is set on fire.

Timber prevents burning in contrast to this! It is achieved by charring on the ground and also forming an adhesive layer that protects the nucleus. Such elements make wood predictable in the event of a fire outbreak. We now know that in this field, wood is doing very well. There is no question that wood is combustible, but there are advantages of structural wood members. Wood joists and studs often resist fire longer than steel, which loses its load-bearing capacity quickly and fails when exposed to heat.

Timber houses must also meet strict requirements for

fire protection. Nonetheless, a modern timber house fulfills them just as quickly as a building constructed of conventional cement frame and masonry forms, even with multiple stories. Wooden structures also have a long and time-honored history: Wood consists of many of the oldest preserved buildings in the world.

The Accusation of Forest Depletion

At the current levels of wood used for power, furniture, paper making, furniture, and design, Dr. Sebastian Pohl of LCEE-Beratungsinstitut sees an "ecological threat." He warns against "wood destruction" and writes that, "The situation of coniferous forests playing critical roles in building, especially spruce, is troublesome." The last German forest inventory showed that consumption was 15 percent higher than the natural rate of regrowth.

These statistics caused consternation in the timber construction industry. More than 120 million cubic meters of new wood expand every year in German forests, based on the record of Denny Ohnesorge, managing director of the German Timber Council (Deutscher Holzwirtschaftsrat). One hundred million cubic meters could be used sustainably, i.e., without reducing standing stocks, but only about 80 million were harvested annually. The German Prefabricated Building Association has found out how much wood is needed to build a prefabricated house. "Growing back in the forests of Germany takes no more than 23 seconds," says its spokesman, Christoph Windscheif.

However, the market share of prefabricated timber houses within Germany varies considerably. Also, it is no accident that the numbers are unusually large in places where there are a lot of trees. "Among coniferous tree species, spruce is a real classic. It is Germany's most common variety, accounting for a quarter of the forests in the state. The wood is at the same time, exceptionally lightweight, robust, and flexible, and it is suitable for making furniture and homes. It is also used in the paper manufacture industry. Also, the biomass of spruce is actually shrinking. Nonetheless, it's not because trees are lost or felled indiscriminately, but because German foresters are slowly, sustainably and efficiently turning fast-growing coniferous forests into mixed stands that reduce monoculture threats."

The Potential Substituting Wood for Mineral-Based Building Materials

The capacity of the oldest building material in the world is significant, especially in preserving the environment on the earth. A detailed scientific study was undertaken at the University of Bochum within the framework of the German Federal Ministry for Environment, Nature Conservation, Infrastructure, Building and Nuclear Safety's Forest Climate Fund has recently confirmed this.

The study includes detailed greenhouse gas balances for wooden houses and factors of replacement that support the tremendous potential of wood production.

One of the conclusions drawn is that to fully leverage this opportunity, the market share for timber construction will have to continue to grow. It is also essential to start replacing timber with mineral-based buildings.

Results

Wood is the only green raw material that emits far less CO_2 than traditional construction materials such as steel, cement, asphalt, brick, and aluminum, when used in its natural form or as processed wood products. It is also the only one to bind and also contain a toxic greenhouse gas, which is carbon dioxide.

Wooden houses have significant advantages in terms of carbon storage, insulation, indoor atmosphere, and the use of green, environmentally friendly building materials over traditional mineral-based buildings. Wood also allows us to breathe more efficiently as a healthy and balanced indoor climate is created. Wood is stunning, flexible, and future-proof in a timeless way. Choices for wood are not always motivated by price; they reflect an attitude much more often than not.

9

WOOD JOINERY

Wood joinery is one of woodworking's most basic concepts. If we are not able to join two pieces of wood together in a stable way, both parts of wood will be sculptures, which are made from a single piece of wood. Nevertheless, a woodworker has several joints in his repertoire to choose from, depending on the task, with several varying forms of wood joinery.

Basic Butt Joint

No more simple wood joinery occurs than the assembly. A butt joint is nothing more than a piece of wood that is fastened into another piece (most often at the right angle or square to the other board), and also fastened with mechanical fasteners. This form of joint is often used on construction sites for wall framing. You can as well read advice on how to use a butt joint and when to pick another type of wood joinery.

Mitered Butt Joint

A mitered butt joint is almost identical to a basic butt joint, except for the fact that the two boards are joined together at an angle (instead of square). The advantage is that there will be no end grain on the mitered butt joint, and as such, it is a little more aesthetically pleasing. Nonetheless, not all the solid is the mitered butt joint.

Half-Lap Joint

The half-lap joint is where half of each of the two boards that are joining is separated so that the two boards are pushed together. This form of wood joinery can compromise the stability of the two adjacent boards, but it is also stronger than the joints of the butt. There are several projects where, given its drawbacks, this sort of wood joint is quite attractive.

Tongue and Groove Joint

When you tie two square boards together along a long edge, you can easily assemble the joint and also keep it together with fasteners. The tongue and groove joint, however, is much smoother and has more adjoining surface areas, which is very useful if the joint is to be glued.

Mortise and Tenon Joint

Mortise and tenon is a traditional method of wood joinery. Since the early days of woodworking, these joins have been used and are still among the best and most sophisticated ways of joining wood. You can also learn how solid, beautiful mortise and tenon joints can be made.

Biscuit Joint

Another way to connect boards along the edges (such as the tongue and groove joint) is to cut holes and use Beechwood wafers (known as biscuits) to keep the boards in place. It is a handy traditional woodworking pair, particularly for creating tabletops, rely on glue and Beechwood biscuit swelling to keep the boards in place. Know how to slice regular slots from biscuit joinery, and you'll get reliable results.

Pocket Joint

The Pocket Joint is a wood joinery style that involves cutting a slot and pre-drilling a pilot hole between two boards at an angle, right before joining the two with a screw. This pre-drilling must be very accurate, so it is usually done using a professional jig. Pocket joints work very well for face frames in the cabinet and other related applications that don't need a lot of strength. Follow the steps in your woodworking projects to build pocket joints.

Dado

A dado is nothing more than a square slot on a board, where a particular piece suits. It is a widely used wood joint for joining plywood, such as building cabinetry, compared to the tongue and groove joinery. Know how to cut a die and when to use it properly.

Rabbet

The rabbet is another typical wood joint used in the cabinetry. A rabbet is a cut along a board's edge. Rabbets are often used to mount the rear to the sides of the container, which is done at the back of cabinets and other similar configurations, giving additional force to the assembly. Know-how and when to use dry rabbets.

Through Dovetail Joint

The most respected by dovetail may be through Dovetail Joint Of all wood joinery methods. A dovetail classic is stunning and very strong, adding a touch of elegance to any piece it's used on. There are few ways to create dovetails, from hand cutting to jig-making. Learn the keys and how to build them through the dovetail joint.

Half-Blind Dovetail Joint

There are cases where the contact of choice is a dovetail pair, but it should not be apparently all sides of the dovetails. A perfect example is a front drawer, where you don't want to see the end of the dovetail on the drawer's head. A semi-blind dovetail is the best choice for this form of joint. Learn how to build a dry, strong, and beautiful semi-blind dovetail joint, and also how to use this wood joinery style.

Sliding Dovetail

A sliding dovetail with many possible uses is a flexible pair. A better way of thinking about it is like dice for locking. Know the keys and when to use one in order to create a secure sliding dovetail joint.

Box Joint

Dovetail joints are beautiful and powerful, but they are not always functional. For the dovetail joint, a box joint is a better option. In your woodworking designs, learn how to build clear and stable box joints.

10

TIMBER CONSTRUCTION SYSTEMS

Nowadays, tall and intricate timber structures can be built technologically. The boundaries of what you can do, even in new projects, have been moved ahead. This progress–plus regulatory changes–creates new ways of inspired and innovative constructions for architects to use wood.

In Sweden, building one and two-story buildings in wood is a very long and proud tradition. Nevertheless, a trend towards taller wooden structures has evolved in recent years. Things are beginning to improve, led by building codes understanding the security, and also the quality strengths of wood and the importance they offer. Wood buildings are now propelling to even higher heights, with innovative technologies such as CLT.

There are several Swedish companies with vast wood background, passed down over generations, enabling them to manage any task with great skill. There are variations in their wood building methods, but also several aspects in general. There can be conventional stud walls or dense floor frameworks within units. In some instances, when it comes to being free, they are subjected to timber limitations. Installation methods in floors and shafts are prepared in advance, while horizontally and vertically noise and fire-proofing separation are taken care of between the buildings.

Buildings of CLT and post and beam structures have the advantage of providing greater flexibility for space configurations, and continuous spans. There are mostly setbacks when it comes to sound insulation effects. Many models include a cast concrete slab of 50 millimeters (1,9 inches) or more, which allows the average thickness of the floor structure to be reduced by about 100 millimeters (3,9 inches)while maintaining the same effect of sound insulation. The thickness of the floor plan not only influences the overall height, but also the façade architecture and alignment of the tower with the built environment around it.

Wood is well known for its ecological qualities–but it also has a wide range of functional properties. It provides thermal insulation, wind, and temperature resistance, resists the effects of friction and compression, and it is easy to handle and form. Wood is also easy to alter and refine, paint and treat, and it has a finished surface prepared for use directly after sawing and preparing. With care and maintenance, the effort placed into the ground is expressed throughout the building's life. Climate, oxidation from the light, dirt, color, and patina of the sun are, in some ways, the best friends of a wooden building–they help to give character and charm over a very long period of time to a wooden façade.

Construction design is often related to modern automobile manufacturing. Competition in both sectors is hard, and consumers' survival depends on the brand being refreshed and tailored to the end customer. A defective service represents a major risk, even to the largest company. A good one has a quality of its own that makes the owner happy. There may be some parallels between manufacturing a house and a car, nonetheless, unlike an automobile, an elegant building can make people happy more than the owner and the consumers. It also helps to increase the quality and prestige of a whole city or district, in tandem with green and energy-efficient buildings.

Derome can use surface units to deliver buildings of up to 6–7 stories, with enormous scope for creative floor plans. Industrially, they build all the wooden frames and also move the units to the building site for quick and efficient assembly. The ground modules are made up of an enclosed wooden structural frame and a surface sheet. It is possible to adapt the façade material to the venue. Derome will launch a new offering in the form of modules of up to four stories shortly.

On the floor, Martinsons uses cross-laminated timber (CLT), and it stabilizes walls, sometimes using the post and beam system. The inside of the outer walls is CLT, which is filled with insulation and the outside façade. The floor structure of the building consists of a CLT panel bonded to glulam beams, with a glulam underlying flange beam with insulation. A frame of 220 millimeters (8,6 inches) of wooden beams is removed from the top of the floor framework that supports the ceiling below. Insulating between the beams is added. The ground structure is about 0.5 meters (19,6 inches) high. The units of the CLT are 12 meters (39,3 feet) long and 1.2 meters (47,2 inches) wide. The units on the floor area are on the wall units of the CLT. The full length of the door is 2 meters (78,7 inches) without being reinforced. The façade openings should be symmetrically spaced along the vertical axis so that enough support can be created by the outer walls.

Moelven Töreboda's in-house design, dubbed Trä8, uses a post and beam solution. It includes glulam posts and columns, a glulam and LVL (Laminated Veneer Lumber) panel stabilizing the device, as well as floors and ceilings using LVL boards and frames. Stability is maintained by glulam and LVL box beam systems, which are packed with separation from mineral fibers. The floor units are built from LVL panels, with most of the veneer layers running at 90 degrees in length. The panels were laid on beams of LVL, with fibers flowing along their length. The exterior can be finished with outer or between the post and the beam carcass curtain walls. When it comes to window selection, the architectural design allows for great freedom.

Lindbäcks Bygg uses wooden box units with a height of 2.5 meters (98,4 inches) and dimensions of max 3.9x 8.4 meters (12,7x 27,5 feet). Road transport limitations decide the maximum length. The modules' outer walls were load-bearing, with the walls supporting the roof and the floor. The modules are designed to allow for two or more modules to shape space. There may also be two or smaller rooms in one unit, such as a toilet, hallway, or closet. If a frame wall is less than 4.4 meters (14,4 feet), glulam beams compensate for gaps, and larger steel joists are used when a wall is used. Stud walls are the walls in the units. For purposes of safety, openings in façades and load-bearing, walls should be placed symmetrically along the vertical axis, which may restrict the choices of the door. On the other hand, in wooden buildings, it is an example of a typical façade style.

11

REASONS WHY YOU SHOULD GO WITH A TIMBER FRAME FOR YOUR BUILDING

For self-builders trying to make decisions that will have an effect on their future home, it can be an overwhelming experience. Generally, one of the main questions is whether to choose a Timber Frame building over a Brick Construction.

It's important to choose the right product for your new home.

And why don't we help? It's not about how great timber kits are; it's about getting you on the building journey. We want to be open and honest with you, and we want to share some of the reasons why our product might be right for you or wrong with you.

Beauty, Warmth, Connection

It's easy to say that any house design has timber frames that bring charm and distinction. While distinctive architectural details uncovered posts and beams, timbered rafters immediately stood out. The strength of personality stood out, which is always compelling for any visitor's admiration and curiosity. Nonetheless, that is not necessarily understood by the unconscious relation. The uncovered timber frame is easy to interpret, making it easier for people to "understand" the house, rather than concealed under drywall and paneling skins. What designers call "size"–the inhabitant's relation to the house–is the opposite of soaring glass skyscrapers!

Better Thermal, Acoustic And Environmental Performance

A timber frame is very flexible, in the sense that it helps you to attach materials that increase both thermal and acoustic quality to your home. Timber frame construction allows you to easily mount items outside the frame, untouched, in order to help protect your home from outside noises and changes of temperature, making it easier and cheaper to sustain a safe, clean, and energy-efficient interior setting.

Fast installation

One of the best factors about timber frame building is that the on-site construction is much smoother, as it's all pre-made. After the foundations have been laid and the package is shipped to the site, in a matter of weeks, a timber frame could go up and be watertight!

No limit on design

Timber frame houses are unique to building people's personal preferences. Therefore, that's why every model is different. How does it feel like a home designed to meet your exact needs? No space sacrifices (as you often have to do with new buildings in the estate). Timber frames offer endless possibilities for development, and they can open more doors for your new construction.

Cost-effective

Such prices are much more stable when operating in a factory setting. Just a few numbers of people in a warehouse can produce a timber kit, as opposed to conventionally 5 or 6 buildings on site. With more people, the company means more overheads.

However, a lot of things can cause delays in the production of bricks, and they can add up to additional costs. The climate, for example, well, if you're lucky enough to live in bonny Scotland, you know how temperamental it can be. The building of timber frames is not based on conditions, so, no delay in your time. Okay, you know what they do say, "time is money."

Reduced construction time

Because the timber frame is made before being shipped to the site in a factory, construction time is much easier, since all the pieces can go together.

The construction time for Timber Frames is greatly reduced due to conventional building methods. So, it's no longer a painfully slow process or brick by brick; it is now a simple and economical solution that will help you move forward faster.

Not weather dependent

Scotland's most wet areas experience an average of 250 days of rain per year, while the driest parts see only about 150 days of rain per year on average. Nevertheless, that doesn't even mention snowfall... That's 40% of the year that the traditional methods for construction can't work and could cause delays to your venture.

Nevertheless, for Timber Frames, the building will continue, regardless of rain or snow.

Sustainable building method

Similar to other construction methods, they use approaches to build a timber package. You know that it's the most environmentally conscious way out there to pick a timber pack. Four quick points on how environmentally friendly timber kits are:

Lowest CO_2 cost of the commercial building method.

Concrete requires five times (and steel uses six times) more energy to produce than wooden frames. Transport costs from the site are smaller as wood is lightweight, which allows less travel back and forth. In addition, the lightness of timber ensures that it can quickly be built using basic tools. This has an enormous impact on how much fuel a venture consumes, generating lower CO_2 buildup.

Less Waste.

Because of the manufacture of timber frames in a factory setting, you have greater control of the waste schemes. Similar to conference construction, the on-site building also has less waste. Less waste, less landfill–the construction of wood frames also help to promote a more sustainable society.

High levels of thermal insulation.

Timber Frames are the eco-friendly present that continues to give thermal insulation. How does a good score for Building Energy sound? Also, how about lower bills for energy? With the construction of a timber frame, you can select the insulation that suits your needs. Using good insulation and membranes can bring down U-values to an all-time decrease. It means saving more and wasting less.

Higher quality

It's all about regulation and performance. This creates something that can often be missed on a normal page.

If it is made in a controlled environment, you will always get a better product value. Building on site is a daunting task, and with frequent works, small items can slip through the cracks. In timber frame building, all of it is prefabricated, so, you have a simple plan in place before you even walk onto the floor.

With better management of performance, materials, and design, you are sure to get three items with the construction of timber frames.

Lightweight structure – strong and durable

Though Timber Frames are regarded as a lightweight design, do not confuse this because they are soft in meaning. Timber frames are extremely strong and long-lasting, with some framed buildings they last with the right care for generations. Also, because Timber frames weigh less, they can be used on brownfield sites or hard-conditioned land.

Construction modern method

Are you the type of person who likes to stay on-trend? Then a timber frame building is the best choice for you.

Timber frames are gaining more potential throughout

the whole UK. And it's no wonder! They're fast building material, with no compromise on quality paired with being eco-friendly. Two things every self-builder wants to be aware of when carrying out a self-build.

Off-site manufacturing

A huge advantage of using a timber frame is that all are manufactured off-site. Once everything has been shipped to the web, everything works like a puzzle. Thanks to the previous planning, a timber frame could go up and be watertight in a matter of weeks.

This saves a lot of time when constructing so that you can get into your new home quite easily.

Easy to Maintain

Similar to other materials, Timber frame homes are cheap and easy to maintain. The maker typically "guarantees" the home design for varying periods. Usually between the period of 10 to 40 years. Nonetheless, as an authority on timber frames, we recommend that you take care of your timber frame. We also suggest a structural review after 5 to 10 years, so that you can have the chance to fix any issues that have arisen.

Several options to restore timber frames are open so that you can get the durability you deserve. Like any house, some maintenance will be required as well.

12

CONSIDERATIONS TO BUILD A TIMBER FRAME HOME

Congratulations, you've decided to build your dreams' timber frame house! So, what can you do to make sure you're building it in the right way? There are seven criteria you can use to make sure that your new home suits your style, budget, and construction needs.

1. Has your timber frame home been appropriately designed?

Building a timber frame home starts with a piece of paper like every venture. Make sure that your designer/engineer/architect/builder has specific experience in the construction of timber frame houses. Their expertise will thereby ensure the proper design of your home to be sturdy, elegant, and also cost less and last longer.

2. Do you want a full timber frame home or just timber accents?

Timbers provide the entire structure of the building in an utterly timber-framed home. It is the most powerful way of building your home. It can cost more than a traditional house, since more timbers will be used. If you don't want a total timber building, you could also choose to build a conventionally framed house with some timber-built sections, either for structural or aesthetic purposes. For example, traditional framing can be applied for all bedrooms, and timbers can be used to offer the support and elegance of wood accents to living rooms, entryways, and trusses.

3. Do you want a timber frame or post and beam frame?

The words timber frame and post and beam are sometimes interchanged, so, it's essential to be clear about what you're looking for. The color of timbers used is the most apparent difference between a timber frame and a post and beam house. Timber frames cut all woods into square posts, while it is usually round for posts and beam posts.

Sections of the frame are assembled on the floor when constructing a timber frame and then raised as whole pieces (called bents) to be set up. The walls and roof are erected over it after the entire timber frame has been completed.

Post and beam homes use first-placed wooden posts, and, due to their weight and length, additional timbers are added one by one.

Today, to create a blended appearance, home designs are beginning to incorporate timber frame and post and beam timbers.

4. Which wood will you use to build your timber frame home?

To ensure that you select the best wood species and method for the layout and construction of your house, you will want to collaborate with your architect and engineer.

Finally, you can choose the type of timber. Oak, fir, spruce, or cedar? Based on the model you like, there are a variety of wood types to choose from. It will rely on your position for their availability and cost. Douglas Fir and Red Cedar, for example, are the most popular options on Canada's west coast, due to their strength and availability.

The way timbers are processed derives from their strength, appearance, and longevity. Dry kiln, wholly planned, focused woods are the luxury choice to create a timber frame house. The most economical option available is rough sawn, green forest, and packed core timbers.

We do not recommend using "yellow wood" as a word of caution. This wood has been dried and is new from the forest. Green timbers have a high content of moisture that can contribute to shifting, change, and also cracking as the age of the building goes up.

5. What joinery will best support your timber frame home?

Two timbers can be joined in more than one way. Power is always the number one goal, and then the option is a matter of beauty.

Engineers always prefer steel joinery and fasteners, because they are stronger and more comfortable to do calculations for. Through hundreds of years of construction, however, wood to wood joinery has proved its strength. Wood to wood joinery means there'll be more labor costs during the process of woodcutting, but fewer material costs since fewer fasteners are required.

When it comes to style: Do you prefer the traditional and natural look of wood to wood joinery? Do you like to see the metal links turn up a little bit? Or do you like natural wood to be compared with metal connectors? Based on the style and budget of your house, you can mix and also match the timber frame home joinery.

6. What's the best framing method for building your home?

Builders may integrate timbers into a building in two different ways.

One is an open timber frame which ensures that the walls are constructed on the timbers' outer surface. This way of the building emphasizes the timbers inside the house, shielding them away from damage by rain, and making them easy to separate and airtight. However, because it is partially covered, it takes away part of the frame's external look. It can be great if you are living in an environment where you have to follow strict rules to what your house would look like on the outside, or if you want a typical outside home look and a wooden frame inside.

The other approach is to build walls between the timbers, which also makes them transparent from outside the building. It is perfect if you want the interior and exterior to have the look and feel of a timber frame. For framing and isolating, this design can require larger timbers.

7. How can you choose a good builder for your timber frame home?

Make sure that the distributor taking your timber frame back to life suits your schedule, expectations, and desires. Keep in mind that a meager price may sacrifice anything and may not always be the best option.

Most importantly, make sure that the contractor can handle your timber frame house as it should look when your dream home is real.

KEY QUESTIONS TO ASK BEFORE HIRING A TIMBER HOME BUILDER

You want to make sure that you get the right team when it comes to hiring a professional home builder to help you build your dream home. We have all heard terrible stories about works that have not been completed to standards, and worse, that has not been finished at all. It's a big investment to recruit a contractor, so you will have the chance to make sure that you protect all your bases and ask the right questions. When hiring a home builder, here are some important questions to ask.

It's a good idea to be ready when you go to see a general contractor for the first time. Below are some key questions you can possibly ask to help you out.

What contracts or homes have you worked on?

The contractor essentially gives you his resume by providing a list of previous jobs. You can check the quality of his previous projects with this information, and get a sense of customer satisfaction. It will also help you build your confidence in the business to see the styles of homes and projects that they have built, and whether there is any comparison with your design.

Have you ever built homes in this geographic

area?

This may sound like a naughty question, but no every log homes are the same, and it's different to build a log home on the coast than building one in the central interior. Experience means that because of its location, your builder will have a knowledge of the local terrain and how to make your home structurally sound.

What type of timbers do you use, and why?

A good builder will have good reasons to stick with the materials we use, giving you both a sense of relief about the building of your house, as well as practical knowledge of the trade.

Are you a licensed carpenter and a member of the local home builders association?

Usually, the answer to this question will be YES. Better presence in a local association is possibly implying competence, knowledge, and, most importantly, happy customers. A good builder is going to want to be in an organization to be able to display their credentials and also advertise.

What are the payment terms?

Nobody likes surprises, so it's important to know if the contractor wants compensation and how much is owed at the project's beginning, middle, and/or at the end. The system can be simplified by a financial officer who knows building loans.

Do Your Own Research

Conduct the company's Google search. Searching through third-party reports and comments should give you a good understanding of the business and its credibility. If in the past, there have been any allegations or questions, odds are they have been filed with an agency, and they may appear in the findings of your search.

Any developer or designer you are considering for your design should be investigated. Besides doing your homework and asking the right questions, you want to make sure that you get along with the vendors with whom you are going to work. You want someone to support you, someone on whom you can rely, someone, you are comfortable talking to about your log home information.

13

STEP-BY-STEP GUIDE TO BUILD YOUR OWN HOUSE

Very few individuals are qualified to take all the steps in building a house, but you may be able to act as your General Contractor (GC), hiring the subcontractors (subs) as anticipated.

There may be some pieces of work that you can do yourself, but by learning the whole system, you can only decide what to do.

This guide explains the principles and the chronology for planning your house-building. Recruiting the subcontractors on an as-you-need-them basis and saving money where you can, by incorporating sweat equity, is the largest single cash-saver when it comes to building a home.

Imagine what goes into a house where an architect is already drawing up plans as the GC in this section.

Site and Construction Basics

Now, it's time, literally and figuratively, to get settled. Not only do you have your project right in your head and on paper, but you're also seated on the building site at your planned residence.

Clear the brush and other debris building site down to ground level, and at least 25 feet (7,6 m) around the perimeter of the proposed home. This often involves a separate work team doing the job.

> The lot is staked by a surveyor, based on original plot sketches showing the borders of the land.

> Make changes to the site's topography when required, in order to change the flow of water to the site. This frequently requires an earth-moving equipment contractor.

> Purchase a roll-off dumpster during the construction project in order to accommodate the refuse.

> Order the power company's emergency supplies.

> Hire a professional electrician to hook up an electrical panel. This is often installed on a *current utility pole.*

Pouring Concrete Footings and Foundation

Things will begin to get intense now with the digging and construction of bases and slabs, both in terms of labor and also in terms of spending money. Before that, it felt like a boring preparatory work; now, you're going to feel like you're constructing something.

Excavation contractors and foundation specialists often do this work— a completely different group of contractors other than the carpentry crews that will be on-site shortly. This is a no return point. Footings and foundation form so much of the expense of your entire house construction that you would have wasted after the foundation is designed. Then, you're going to have a huge amount of cement and masonry work cluttering a site, making it extremely difficult to sell the property.

Here's What Happens

You or the contractor will be needed to bring in a separate company with the single purpose of building foundations, as the job requires very specialized skills.

> ➢ For ice footings, the builder builds trenches.

> ➢ Inspectors come to test the foot trenches' sizes.

> ➢ For footings, the builder pours cement.

> ➢ Footing drains are built and also designed to drain and protect water from the footers.

> ➢ The builder uses either poured concrete or concrete cinder blocks to create vertical

foundation walls laying on the footings. Certain forms of foundations, while uncommon, are sometimes used.

➤ The base is durable up to the level that it gets finished. In the foundation wall, holes are created to allow water supply and drain lines to be routed.

Running Plumbing and Electrical Lines

When you lay a slab-type foundation, some of the utilities will be "rough-in" by plumbers and electricians before paving the concrete slab:

➤ Plumbers: Tubes will be laid down and will finally be filled with cement.

➤ Electricians: When electrical lines run through the concrete slab through metal pipes, the time has come to fire these pipes.

Pouring the Concrete Slabs

It's time for the subcontractor to mix the cement with everything in place.

➤ The manufacturer must first install concrete foam board insulation on a house floor.

➤ A minimal gravel foundation of four inches slides over the foam board, creating the concrete base.

> First is a door of polymer smoke.

> The reinforcement of the wire mesh is then laid down and placed, so it is slightly higher than the level. This will cause the reinforcement to sit in the middle of the concrete surface, providing the most reinforcement of energy.

> The company is now mixing the concrete slab, possibly from ready-mix trucks carrying a large amount of cement.

> If you're building a garage or cellar, it's time to dump cement in those areas as well. Bringing the concrete company out to another pour is really costly.

Framing, Siding, and Roofing

You will quickly begin to recognize your home as a house when the digging, base, and concrete work are done. This is because the framing carpenters will now arrive to install the framework lumber for the floors, ceilings, walls, and then move to the siding, and roofing installation. At an incredible pace, this work can be carried out. You may notice your home as a building within a week or two.

At this point, some homeowners can assist with the work, although a skilled carpenter crew will absolutely do this work. Nevertheless, some homeowners may tackle sections of the work, such as laying the floor sheathing over the joists or hanging wallboards.

Here is the general factor for the carpentry crew.

Employ a framing order based on your building plans of the necessary wood, nails, felt builder or house cover, and adhesives.

When the weather is good, the carpentry team comes to build the walls of the house, including the foundation of the floor, ceiling, and roof. Framing is the house's simple frame, minus the siding and the top of the roof. At this time, the rough spaces will be framed for windows, doors, and skylights. Each phase is completed by the simple sheathing of the wall and the roof surfaces.

The curtains, doors, and skylights should be mounted. In most cases, the same carpentry team who did the construction will do this, although sometimes, the crew of a company will come in to do the job. It is also a task that can be tackled by some homeowners. At this point, when the house is enclosed, and doors and windows are mounted, the subcontractors doing the electrical and plumbing work can now come in to begin the difficult portion of their job.

After the house sheathing is first covered with some weather guard membrane, the finished side layer is now mounted over the sheathing. Also, the same person that did the painting and sheathing often does this job.

Finally, the roofers come into full roof bursts or shingles, or other completed roof surfaces. The house's simple shell is now finished.

Installation of Rough-In Electrical and Plumbing

With the presence of masons, electricians, plumbers, and HVAC technicians, the interior construction on your house can now begin.

If your home has one, the masons build the chimney. This usually involves applying brick or stone veneer to a concrete block base that the foundation contractor laid down.

The rough-in work done by electricians and plumbers is electrical circuits, drainage tubes, and ductwork of the HVAC system. This function is simpler without the textures on the ground, floor, and ceiling. Upon completion, these contractors will leave for a while, and they'll return to complete the final connections of different fixtures after the walls and ceilings are in order.

There are rough-in checks. The company will

manage the process of permits and audits, but if you proceed with this job yourself, you will be responsible for the inspections.

Insulate the walls and the attic. The carpenter company or a specialist contractor sometimes does this, but many homeowners consider that this is a job they can do to save money.

Hanging Drywall and Installing Trim

In the next few measures, as wall and ceiling panels are built, the interior should begin to look completed.

Some homeowners can take these steps on their own, provided they have good DIY skills. If not, there is a crew of finishing carpenters, typically part of the same subcontractor group that supplied the framing carpentry work, who frequently perform this start-up finishing work. The interior finally begins to look like a real interior. Here's the standard job order.

Drywall is hanging all over the room. Before any further work continues, all wall and ceiling surfaces are usually hung.

The edges of the drywall are rubbed, muddled with the joint compound, and then sanded to the edge.

Walls and ceilings of the interior are put out. This is often achieved with spraying equipment, which works easily, because there is no need to think about trimming moldings or ground surfaces.

All interior moldings, including door and window enclosures, as well as crown moldings, are mounted.

In bathrooms, kitchens, and other areas, all cabinets are hung.

Painting and Finish Work

It's time to bring the artist out after the hard job of assembling drywall and priming the walls gets done.

Walls are painted, and either polished or textured ceilings are completed. Also, these are homeowners' tasks that can be solved to save money.

The countertops for the kitchen and bathroom are to be set, and the finish carpenters, homeowners, or specialists in the cabinet and countertop can do this.

Installation and hook-up of completed plumbing and electrical appliances are then completed. Since code problems are present here, this should only be done by the most professional DIYers.

Installing Flooring

Your home's interior is now near completion. There are still a few things needed:

Lay down all the needed items all over the house flooring surfaces of the build. These may include carpeting, hardwood flooring, laminate flooring, ceramic tile, etc. This is often a task for another subcontractor, while homeowners may attempt some flooring construction as well.

Sweep up the place of service, that's the intent of your dumpster. If you choose not to do this yourself, after construction work, there are firms that you can employ that specialize in cleaning up.

Installing Driveway and Landscaping

The last step in your DIY house-building project includes exterior labor, as well as some red tape to clear up.

Total landscaping of the grounds. This can be a DIY's project occasionally, but many companies can model and also build a trendy landscape for you. This is a tedious job but think carefully before you take it on yourself.

To pick up the dumpster, contact the recycling service and inform them that you don't need a replacement.

If you are using a general contractor, plan a final walk-through. When you act as your supplier, after each trade (subcontractor) has done its job, you must "walk-through."

CONCLUSION

We all dream of owning a spacious and modern-looking house that will be built in a short period of time. Nonetheless, it can be a little difficult to fit all this into a mediocre budget. Using timber frames to build your house is a simple solution to this. Such structures typically use thick timbers that are 15 to 30 cm thick for the construction of any structure's basic interior frame. As frame structures designed in the nineteenth and twentieth centuries are still solid, it is a tested and trusted method. The old system is combined with new technology, and it is used to create highly durable structures, using the new streamlined process.

The use of timber frames to build your house has various advantages. One of the biggest advantages is that they are very easy to build. As far as architecture is concerned, there is a lot of flexibility involved, and you can also model your house according to your own custom needs. The construction process takes less time than other traditional construction methods. Once the paper model is ready, and the frame is accepted, it can be as small as one day. Such frame houses have excellent insulation. That panel is fitted with an insulating material, which in cold weather, provides effective insulation. The lightweight frames allow the house to easily adapt to changing environmental conditions, and timber's cooling nature provides better air circulation, keeping the house cool in warmer conditions.

Timber frame houses are very sturdy and are capable of handling any form of weather. For comparison with wooden frames that use screws, they use mortice or tenon joints. Many modern ones also have steel joints offering extended robustness. These are ideal in areas where conditions on the ground do not allow deep foundations to be dug. It helps to save a lot of money, as well as time since it does not entail heavy foundation excavation. Timber can last for decades and it is extremely durable. It is environmentally friendly and also helps to reduce greenhouse emissions by providing better ventilation, thereby reducing energy consumption. It's a completely organic and non-toxic. A typical house saves as much as 4 tons of carbon dioxide as other traditional houses.

Timber frame houses are friendly to the environment. They are highly durable and are also robust, and they can be tailored to individual requirements. So, the best way to do that is if you're planning to build a house timber frame, they're going to save money and provide superior construction options for you. They are very comfortable, and they help to save a great deal of energy and water resources. They are, therefore, ideal retirement homes where you can live in peace and comfort. There are several building companies using timber frames, and a bit of internet research can help you find one that suits your field.

ACKNOWELEDGEMENTS

This work would not have been possible without all of those with whom I have had the pleasure to work during this project.

I would especially like to thank my dear fellow Bob Maison for his constant encouragement and patience.

Nobody has been more important to me in the pursuit of this project than the members of my family.

I would like to thank my parents, whose love and guidance are with me in whatever I pursue.

Most importantly, I wish to thank my loving and supportive wife, Chris, and my three wonderful children, Oscar, Lucy and Sylvia who provide unending inspiration.

CPSIA information can be obtained
at www.ICGtesting.com
Printed in the USA
LVHW031713050120
642559LV00016B/1343/P